POBLACHT NA

THE PROVISIONAL GOVERNMENT

OF THE

IRISH REPUBLIC

TO THE PEOPLE OF IRELAND.

IRISHMEN AND IRISHWOMEN : In the name of God and of the dead generations from which she receives her old tradition of nationhood, Ireland, through us, summons her children to her flag and strikes for her freedom.

Having organised and trained her manhood through her secret revolutionary organisation, the Irish Republican Brotherhood, and through her open military organisations, the Irish Volunteers and the Irish Citizen Army, having patiently perfected her discipline, having resolutely waited for the right moment to reveal itself, she now seizes that moment, and, supported by her exiled children in America and by gallant allies in Europe, but relying in the first on her own strength, she strikes in full confidence of victory.

We declare the right of the people of Ireland to the ownership of Ireland, and to the unfettered control of Irish destinies, to be sovereign and indefeasible. The long usurpation of that right by a foreign people and government has not extinguished the right, nor can it ever be extinguished except by the destruction of the Irish people. In every generation the Irish people have asserted their right to national freedom and sovereignty; six times during the past three hundred years they have asserted it in arms. Standing on that fundamental right and again asserting it in arms in the face of the world, we hereby proclaim the Irish Republic as a Sovereign Independent State, and we pledge our lives and the lives of our comrades-in-arms to the cause of its freedom, of its welfare, and of its exaltation among the nations.

The Irish Republic is entitled to, and hereby claims, the allegiance of every Irishman and Irishwoman. The Republic guarantees religious and civil liberty, equal rights and equal opportunities to all its citizens, and declares its resolve to pursue the happiness and prosperity of the whole nation and of all its parts, cherishing all the children of the nation equally, and oblivious of the differences carefully fostered by an alien government, which have divided a minority from the majority in the past.

Until our arms have brought the opportune moment for the establishment of a permanent National Government, representative of the whole people of Ireland and elected by the suffrages of all her men and women, the Provisional Government, hereby constituted, will administer the civil and military affairs of the Republic in trust for the people.

We place the cause of the Irish Republic under the protection of the Most High God, Whose blessing we invoke upon our arms, and we pray that no one who serves that cause will dishonour it by cowardice, inhumanity, or rapine. In this supreme hour the Irish nation must, by its valour and discipline and by the readiness of its children to sacrifice themselves for the common good, prove itself worthy of the august destiny to which it is called.

Signed on Behalf of the Provisional Government,

THOMAS J. CLARKE.

SEAN Mac DIARMADA.   THOMAS MacDONAGH,

P. H. PEARSE,   EAMONN CEANNT.

JAMES CONNOLLY.   JOSEPH PLUNKETT.

SIGNATORIES

EMMA DONOGHUE · THOMAS KILROY · HUGO HAMILTON
FRANK McGUINNESS · RACHEL FEHILY · ÉILÍS NÍ DHUIBHNE
MARINA CARR · JOSEPH O'CONNOR

SIGNATORIES

ELIZABETH O'FARRELL · PADRAIG PEARSE · JAMES CONNOLLY
ÉAMONN CEANNT · THOMAS CLARKE · SEÁN MAC DIARMADA
THOMAS MacDONAGH · JOSEPH MARY PLUNKETT

UNIVERSITY COLLEGE DUBLIN PRESS
PREAS CHOLÁISTE OLLSCOILE BHAILE ÁTHA CLIATH

2016

First Published 2016
University College Dublin Press
Belfield
Dublin 4
Ireland
© the authors, 2016
ISBN 978-1-910820-10-0

CPI data available from the British Library.

Typeset in Bembo.
Text design and setting by Origin Creative.
Printed in England on acid-free paper
by Anthony Rowe, Chippenham, Wiltshire.

· CONTENTS ·

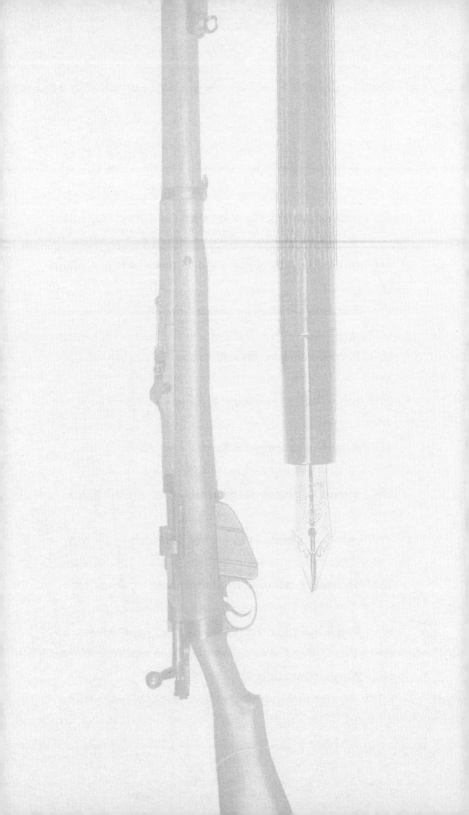

PREFACE

It was while I was sitting in the Common Room in UCD's
Newman Building over a cup of tea with Frank McGuinness,
that the idea of a collaborative literary response to the 1916
Rising came to us. Then and there we hatched a plan to create
a piece of theatre that would truly make history.

We were talking about the University's involvement in the
independence movement through organisations such as the Gaelic
League, the Irish Volunteers and Cumann na mBan, when the
subject of the signatories of the Proclamation came up. In 1916
Thomas MacDonagh was a lecturer in English at UCD, and his
close involvement in the military planning of the Rising reinforced
it as a 'poets' revolution'. What better way to tell the stories of
these leaders than by harnessing the unique power of theatre?

We speak of James Joyce as the father of the modern novel,
and are rightly proud that he is a graduate of our university.
His work is not the only contribution to UCD's literary legacy
however. The university has a remarkable creative tradition, the
true extent of which was brought to light when we celebrated
our 150th anniversary in 2004. At that time, Professor Anthony
Roche edited *The UCD Aesthetic*, a series of twenty-eight essays
on poets, playwrights and authors who have, as he recalled,
'passed through its portals (and continue to do so).' In this
rich collection we find Joseph O'Connor writing about John

McGahern, Katy Hayes reflecting on Neil Jordan, Colm Tóibín responding to the work of Anthony Cronin while Cronin himself writes on Flann O'Brien – a constellation of poetry and prose, drama, fiction and film.

Not long afterwards, in 2007, as UCD made its final move from Earlsfort Terrace to Belfield, we decided to host a series of events to bid 'Farewell to the Terrace'. Originally intending to hold talks in Newman House and a few tours of the old halls of Earlsfort Terrace with an expected audience of several hundred, we had to close the list when the registrations reached 5,000. Clearly the depth of affection for the *alma mater* amongst graduates called for something on a larger scale. The former Great Hall at Earlsfort Terrace is now home to the National Concert Hall, so it was an obvious step to stage a concert. As our tradition lies in the written word rather than music, we created a literary concert with recent UCD graduate writers bringing the work of earlier UCD figures to life: Thomas Kilroy took to the stage to read from Mary Lavin's fiction, Marie Heaney recited Dorothy Molloy, and Gerard Stembridge read from James Joyce's work. The concert remains a highlight in the University's cultural history.

Almost a decade after this event, the creative profile of our alumni remains as strong as ever. Once we had formulated the idea of *Signatories*, Frank brought Patrick Mason on board. An honorary UCD man, Patrick embraced the project and with the wealth of talent on our graduate roll we were soon gathering a line-up of exceptional writers who were willing to take on this unusual and challenging project. In *Signatories* eight of these writers respond to a single brief – to take a named character from this pivotal point in Irish history and to craft what Patrick Mason termed an 'artistic response'. Thomas Kilroy first graduated from UCD in 1956 and, as the doyen among the writers, it was entirely fitting to ask him to take on Pearse. Seven of the writers were assigned a signatory each, and Emma Donoghue was asked to respond to Elizabeth O'Farrell – one of three women who remained in the GPO until the end of the Rising and who delivered the surrender to the British.

From the beginning we wanted the first performance to be at Kilmainham Gaol. The setting is so evocative – entering the cold corridors we immediately think of the despair it must have instilled in those imprisoned there. For the signatories it was a point of no return. The tiny cells were to be the last place they would write their letters, lay their heads and think of their loved ones.

Kilmainham is where we began, but the nature of the monologues – the symphonic movement through sound and tempo, the focus on the voice and the face of the actor – ensure that the play can be performed anywhere.

We set out to captivate the audience but of course we were also motivated by our students, past and present – and by students of Irish literature around the world – who would appreciate this remarkable convergence of politics and art. *Signatories* provides students with the opportunity to explore how different contemporary writers interpret our history and convey something of the very essence of being Irish. Contextualising the past to offer understanding of our present in order to inspire our future – both performance and printed text offer a unique engagement with our cultural moment and our history and, we hope, an enjoyable experience for audience and reader alike.

Because of the close links between UCD and the formation of the Irish State, we are perfectly placed to contextualise 1916 for the current generation of students, to contribute towards their understanding of that period, and offer a mature reflection on past events for Ireland's global audience. *Signatories* takes us beyond the realm of history and political science into the space of cultural experience. It is contemporary and creative, a truly fitting legacy of the centenary of the Rising.

I have many people to thank – first and foremost Frank McGuinness and Patrick Mason for sticking with the project in spite of many challenges. I'm deeply grateful to Marina Carr, Emma Donoghue, Rachel Fehily, Hugo Hamilton, Thomas Kilroy, Éilís Ní Dhuibhne and Joseph O'Connor for entering into the spirit of adventure and creating this wonderful piece of theatre. Thanks to Frank, Patrick, James Ryan and Miriam Hederman O'Brien for bringing the writers on board. I'm grateful to Tony Roche and Lucy Collins in the School of English, Drama and Film, and to Diarmaid Ferriter and Conor Mulvagh in the School of History, for practical assistance along the way. Thanks to Orla Feely, Chair of the UCD Decade of Centenaries Committee, and Professor Andrew Deeks, President of UCD, for ongoing support for this and our other public commemoration projects. My heartfelt thanks to Mary

Staunton, Éamonn Ceannt, Martin Higgins, Fionnan Sheahan and Donal Shiels who repeatedly boosted my determination to bring this project to completion.

In its first production run, *Signatories* opens in Kilmainham Gaol before moving to the Pavilion Theatre, Dún Laoghaire; the Civic Theatre, Tallaght and then to the National Concert Hall for a fitting return to Earlsfort Terrace. In putting together this programme we were supported by Brendan Kenny of Dublin City Council, Tim Carey of Dún Laoghaire Rathdown County Council, Simon Taylor of the National Concert Hall and by John McMahon and Frank Shalvey of the Office of Public Works.

This beautiful book is thanks to Noelle Moran and Damien Lynam of UCD Press and Daniel Morehead of Origin Design, together with Lucy Collins, UCD School of English, Drama and Film. What a pleasure it has been to entrust this volume to their care.

Eilis O'Brien
University College Dublin
April 2016

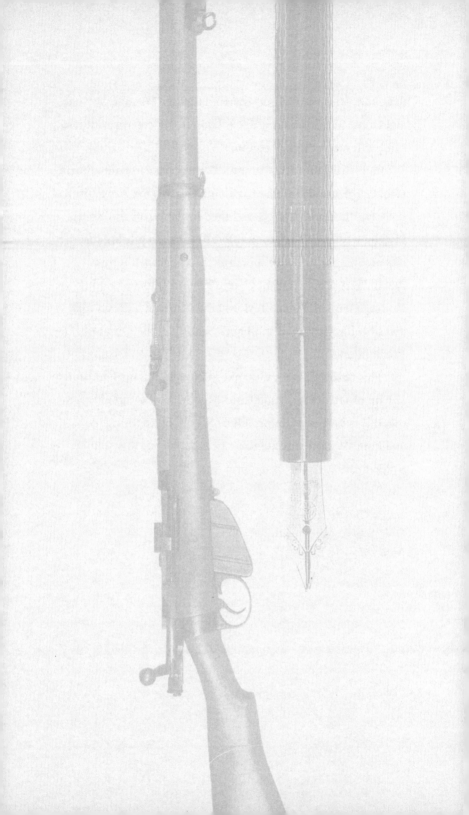

A DIRECTOR'S NOTE

Signatories is a work of theatre consisting of eight monologues, written by eight writers, in response to eight figures from the Easter Rising of 1916. These eight figures are: the seven signatories of the Proclamation of the Irish Republic, and Elizabeth O'Farrell, one of three Red Cross nurses, members of Cumann na mBan, who remained with the insurgents in the GPO, and the woman who helped broker their eventual surrender to the British forces.

The eight writers, all with strong links to UCD, were commissioned by the college in the summer of 2015 to write these short dramatic monologues for performance in the centennial year of 2016. I was subsequently approached by UCD in the autumn of 2015 to direct the first production of *Signatories* the following spring.

1.

The dramatic monologue is an austere and demanding form: it limits the dramatist to the use of a single voice, a single action, a single image. It is true to say that these are the basic building blocks of any drama, but there is one important limitation imposed in the monologue: the vital element of interaction is missing. Any possibility of action being played out between different characters has been removed. The only 'other' available to the writer is the audience itself. And, in the case of this particular commission, a further limitation was imposed: no monologue was to be longer than twelve minutes in duration.

Another potential limitation presented itself in the disparate nature of each voice and each image included. The monologues were all linked by their connection, direct or oblique, to the events of 1916: but each monologue had a distinct tone, and each had a very distinctive take on those events – as distinctive as the individual characters and writers involved. In many ways, though, this diversity has proved to be a major strength of the whole project.

Another strength of the monologue form lies in the intensity of focus it produces on the individual figure portrayed, and in the extreme compression of its emotional energy in performance. It enables the actor to engage in a direct and forceful encounter with the audience, uninhibited by any convention of a 'fourth wall'.

But, whatever the singular force of each dramatic statement, I was puzzled and intrigued as to how eight such different elements could be bound together into an effective piece of theatre with a purposeful sense of dramatic development – an inevitable and dynamic movement from a beginning, through a middle, to an end.

The key to the eventual shape of the production was handed to me by Emma Donoghue's haunting, and haunted, monologue for Elizabeth O'Farrell. In it she creates a

'dream journey' made by Elizabeth in old age, retracing
her courageous criss-crossing of the city that April day to
deliver Pearse's order of surrender. It occurred to me that the
production itself could be such a journey: it could represent
a series of encounters made within a performance space, that
enabled the audience to connect the separate characters, just as
Elizabeth had connected the disparate rebel outposts on that
nightmare day.

Following this idea through, I saw that the performance
could take the shape of a promenade production, with the
audience moving from meeting to meeting, gathering,
dispersing, and re-gathering as the events of the Rising and
its aftermath unfolded in, and through, a sequence of intense
theatrical encounters.

2.

With this idea of the production as a journey re-enacted, I
realised the need for a performance space that would not only
accommodate such a pilgrimage, but would also enhance its
progress. This led me to consider placing the entire action of
the production in Kilmainham Gaol. Easier said than done.

But the idea gathered more and more support over the
months and, after a long and sometimes difficult negotiation
between UCD and the Office of Public Works, we were given
leave to stage *Signatories* in the East Wing of the prison. We
are acutely aware of the privilege of such a permission, and the
responsibilities that go with it.

Following Elizabeth O'Farrell from the smouldering ruins of the GPO, out across the devastated city, a narrative began to emerge from the individual encounters represented in the eight monologues: a story that led from insurrection to surrender, from imprisonment and court martial to execution in the Breaker's Yard in Kilmainham. Other thematic links began to emerge, as well.

Elizabeth O'Farrell stands at Padraig Pearse's side for the surrender, and the perplexing figure of Pearse, so brilliantly caught by Thomas Kilroy, leads us inevitably to Connolly and his political legacy, so surprisingly and effectively illustrated by Hugo Hamilton.

The sharp mix of the political and the personal in Hamilton's young Irish woman leads us, in turn, to the deep humanity of Frank McGuinness's portrait of Éamonn Ceannt. The clash of the humane and the ideological brings us to Thomas Clarke's passionate Fenianism, so robustly recorded by Rachel Fehily, which is then echoed so darkly and effectively in Éilís Ní Dhuibhne's tantalising glimpse of Seán Mac Diarmada, as seen through the eyes of his confused fiancée.

The naiveté of the young Min Ryan yields to the measured maturity of Marina Carr's deeply impressive and wise Thomas MacDonagh, who, in turn, brings us to the charm and pathos of Joseph O'Connor's moving portrait of Joseph Mary Plunkett, the romantic revolutionary and public school boy – and the last of four men to be executed by firing squad on the morning of the 4th of May, 1916: 'You can imagine that, I expect. Hearing the others. Not pleasant.'

More connecting strands began to emerge as the individual voices resounded in my imagination. There was, implicit in the eight monologues, an exhilarating and musical mixture of male and female voices: the 'Irishmen and Irishwomen' evoked by the Proclamation itself. So, through the emerging narrative and thematic sequence I had discovered, I began to hear a developing counter-point of men's tones and women's tones, weaving its way through the journey of the production.

And with this criss-crossing of genders, there also emerged a strange mixing of generations: of the dead generations of the Proclamation and its authors, and of the living generations of the audience, moving from stage to stage through the gaol, and the actors who peopled the performance space.

All these considerations of narrative, theme, music, contrast, and connection, finally came together to determine the particular sequence in which the monologues were to be performed – a sequence that is replicated in the order in which they are printed in this book.

Although performed in an historic building, these monologues are not historical documents. Neither are they acts of national piety. They are acts of theatre – imagined, artistic responses to people and events of the past. All such acts of imagination, like all acts of commemoration, are complex, fraught, and, inevitably, to be contested. But they are a vital part of the way in which we seek to grasp the significance of our history, and the meaning of our modern nation.

3.

The only reason for re-visiting the past, as Brian Friel once put it, is to try and understand where we are in the present. The imagination of the writers engaged in creating this series of performances leads us in many unexpected directions, to many insights and unsettling questions about where we are, and how we got here. Theirs is an idiosyncratic and oblique glance at the past, made through a multitude of different lenses. 'Tell all the Truth but tell it slant,' Emily Dickinson wrote: this collection of dramatic monologues does just that – making the familiar strange, and the strange familiar, as all good theatre should.

Patrick Mason
April 2016

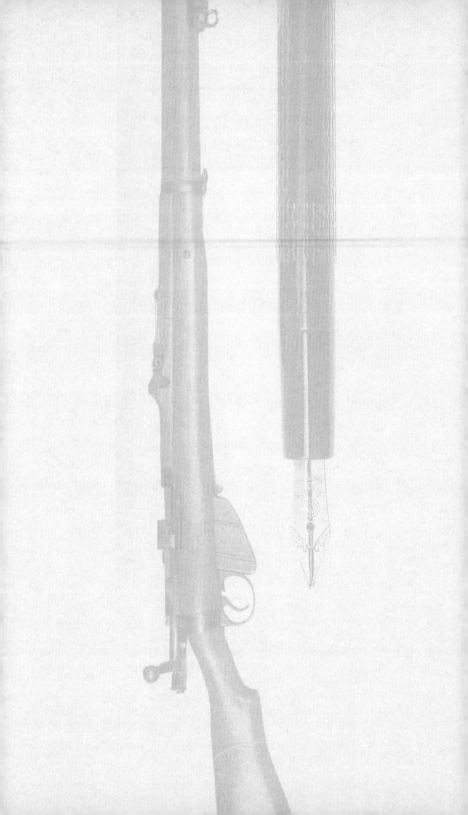

IMAGINING 1916
WRITING AND MEMORY

The Easter Proclamation is a landmark text in Ireland's history.
Printed secretly in the days before the 1916 Rising, it set out
aspirations to freedom and equality that were 'revolutionary'
in the true sense of the word – they imagined a new society
that could only be built in an independent, democratic state.
The seven signatories of the document were men of different
backgrounds and ideologies, yet they had one thing in
common: the commitment to armed insurrection as a means
to realise this new Ireland. As a group, these men constituted
a network of differing yet interlocking aims, uniting Ireland's
revolutionary history with new social and educational
ideals, and disseminating these through the lively literary
and publishing culture of the time. The rebel leaders were
remarkable for their energy and persistence, but they were also
representative figures, carrying the efforts and aspirations of the
many men and women active in cultural and political circles in
the early years of the twentieth century.

So it is fitting that, for this creative work, the voice of a
woman is added to those of the signatories to the Proclamation.
For a decade before the Rising took place, Elizabeth O'Farrell
was a committed member of a number of organisations,
including the Gaelic League and Cumann na mBan. As nurse
and courier, she played a key role in the GPO during Easter

week, tending the wounded and carrying messages across
the city. She was perfectly placed to reflect on the complex
relationship between the leaders of the rebellion and those
who served alongside them. Her voice – the first to be heard
in the performance and to appear in the pages of this book –
describes an act of venturing forth, real in its consequences but
also symbolic of the risk-taking that shaped the events of Easter
week. Her decisive action in communicating the surrender to
each garrison shows the significance of culmination, as well as
of action: 'How long it takes,' she remarks, 'how complicated
it is, to end a war.' So this piece of theatre begins at the end of
the Rising, highlighting acts of remembrance and reflection.
O'Farrell's personal recollections were to be the most enduring
of all – she was not among those executed and her story is not
told in the shadow of death but in acknowledgment of the gift,
and the burden, of survival.

Memory preserves, but also recreates, the events of our past;
every recollection of the Rising defines its later representation,
by inclusion or omission. Our understanding of these events is
shaped by collective memory, but also by impression, anecdote
and representation. The close links between the Easter Rising
and the Irish cultural revival provide a rich artistic legacy
within which the events of Easter week can be viewed. This
network of texts and associations emphasises the shared
purpose of the time and the necessity of acknowledging the
many perspectives of participants and witnesses. O'Farrell's
memories of the women to whom she was closest, personally

and politically, not only retrieve these lives – so long obscured in official histories – but also highlight the imaginative power of shared sacrifice. Together, these monologues express both the intensity of individual experience and the unbreakable bonds of human solidarity and affection.

In the decades following the Rising, popular perception may have sanctified the rebel leaders, but the uniqueness of each man's temperament and motivation was first revealed in his own words. All were writers: in memoirs, essays, plays and poems they explored their ideas and often reflected directly on how these would be received by readers. Re-imagining the revolutionaries one hundred years later, today's writers reveal not only the complexity of these characters but also how each has been understood through the texts of the past. Each contemporary writer brings a unique perspective to the recreation of history; these creative responses will enter our collective memory, inspiring, in their turn, new processes of imagination and reflection. The significance of language as a means of shaping the flux of experience is explicitly considered: as the figure of Pearse reflects, 'nothing has ever happened until it is written down'. No book can fully capture the performance process, but here the language of thought and emotion are given lasting form.

The Proclamation was largely Pearse's work and it was he who read it outside the GPO on 24 April 1916. Pearse's path to revolutionary leadership was a winding one; his monologue emerges from the twin emotions of fear and desire, at once expressing and transcending these feelings. The duality of his thought can be traced in his character and circumstances – born of an English father and an Irish mother, Pearse was deeply committed to the Irish language tradition but drew inspiration from European education. His idealism was balanced by a fierce work ethic; his yearning for blood sacrifice finally tempered by the reality of violence. Such apparent contradictions exemplify the many strands of Irish political and cultural life during these years, at times tightly interwoven, at times unravelling to reveal distinct and conflicting positions. Pearse's capacity to give voice to, yet transcend, strong ideological convictions is a source of imaginative strength, both for the man himself and for the generations that memorialised him.

It is the inspirational quality of the Rising, as much as its historical fact, which ensures its foundational significance for modern Irish identity. If the executed rebels were buried in unmarked graves, their names nonetheless lived on. Songs and poems commemorated their achievements, and these are given voice in this production: 'A Nation Once Again' punctuates Thomas Clarke's thoughts, linking him to the radical nationalism of Thomas Davis in the 1840s, while 'Brian Boy Magee' draws its inspiration from the 1641 Rebellion. This particular poem offers an oblique illumination of Seán Mac Diarmada's work promoting republicanism in Ulster. Interwoven with Min Ryan's recollections of Mac Diarmada, with whom she was romantically involved, the poem grounds this representation in an interactive scene, its brutality offering an eerie counterpart to the subdued prison visit that Min and her sister Phyllis made before the executions began.

The effect of these executions was to generate support for the rebels and widespread respect for their heroism. These responses extended beyond those who were close to the men, revealing the lasting impact of their ideals as well as their actions. The life of James Connolly is refracted here through the story of a later generation of Irish emigrants, still challenged by mistreatment and marginalisation. Connolly himself came from such a community and his dedication to an independent Ireland was a commitment to a better future for all working people. His intellect was shaped by collective need and is fittingly expressed not in the intense experience of his own wounding and death, but through troubling domestic scenes. The fragility of home and family, contemplated in this monologue, shadows the sequence as a whole. For men on the eve of execution, the comfort of home can only be relived in memory, yet its symbolic importance – as signified by Éamonn Ceannt's concluding words – rests on the dignity it confers on a dispossessed people; it is the space in which self-governance and freedom can be realised by the individual.

1916 is often termed a 'poets' rebellion', since three of the seven signatories of the Proclamation were published poets. Thomas MacDonagh, a scholar and lecturer at University College Dublin, was influenced by both Irish and English literary traditions. For him lasting freedom was linked to morality: love, not enmity, was at the centre of his philosophy. His capacity to empathise with his own executioners dramatises this breadth of vision and reveals his potential for self-reflection.

He was a man, as W. B. Yeats put it in 'Easter, 1916', who was 'coming into his force'. The last word here belongs to another poet, though. Joseph Mary Plunkett's lyrical reflections echo his own writings, but are tempered by wit and a momentary detachment that allows him to speak to the future as well as to the present. In linking the Ireland of his own experience with the country of today, Plunkett's monologue crosses temporal boundaries. Dwelling on the brevity of his marriage, he sheds light on the limited time we all have for momentous action. The theatre of revolution, just like that of commemoration, is soon over, but its meanings live on.

Lucy Collins
University College Dublin
April 2016

Dictionary of Irish Biography. 9 vols. Cambridge: Cambridge University Press with the Royal Irish Academy, 2009.

Ferriter, Diarmaid. *A Nation and Not a Rabble: The Irish Revolution 1913–1923.* London: Profile Books, 2015.

Foster, R. F. *Vivid Faces: The Revolutionary Generation in Ireland, 1890–1923.* New York: Norton, 2015.

Higgins, Roisín. *Transforming 1916: Meaning, Memory and the Fiftieth Anniversary of the Easter Rising.* Cork: Cork University Press, 2012.

Kiberd, Declan and P. J. Mathews, eds. *Handbook of the Irish Revival: An Anthology of Irish Cultural and Political Writings 1891–1922.* Dublin: Abbey Theatre Press, 2015.

McDiarmid, Lucy. *At Home in the Revolution: What Women Said and Did in 1916.* Dublin: Royal Irish Academy, 2015.

McGarry, Fearghal. *The Rising: Ireland, Easter 1916.* Oxford: Oxford University Press, 2016.

Martin, F. X., ed. *The Easter Rising 1916 and University College Dublin.* Dublin: Browne and Nolan, 1966.

Townshend, Charles. *Easter 1916: The Irish Rebellion.* London: Penguin, 2005.

White, Lawrence William and James Quinn, eds. *1916: Portraits and Lives.* Dublin: Royal Irish Academy, 2015.

ELIZABETH O'FARRELL

SIGNATORIES

EMMA DONOGHUE

ELIZABETH O'FARRELL

BY

EMMA DONOGHUE

Elizabeth O'Farrell checks her pocket watch.

A quarter to one, Saturday the 29th of April. The Temporary Headquarters of the Provisional Leadership of the Irish Republic, one of Moore Street's score of fishmongers, poulterers, butchers. The place reeks of blood and guts.

She hoists her improvised white flag and takes a step forward.

In my dreams now I walk out that door again, over and over, ready for the bullet that's got my name on it. No, not ready, you can't ever be ready, all you can do is make a shield of your fear, and it's not the kind of shield that blocks bullets either. All it does is keep me upright, stepping forward into whatever's already aiming for me.

She waves the flag. Walks forward, step by step.

Flag held high but not in pride. White for peace, but this is capitulation. White for innocence, ha!

My shoulders are aching already. Moore Street's littered with slates, lumps of masonry the size of my skull. I pick my way through, watching out for unexploded shells. The soldiers are firing from their barricade of furniture across the top of the street. Bullet!

She ducks, then stands straight.

Not mine. Not this time. Is this rag no use at all?

I don't flatter myself: Commandant Pearse chose me to deliver
his message because a man would be shot right away, no matter
the colour of his flag. Which doesn't mean that I won't be
shot, it only tilts the odds. I've a red cross on the bib of my
apron and another on my sleeve, but that's only camouflage.
Yes, I'm a nurse in training, but I don't belong to the Red
Cross: I'm an insurgent. A despatcher, a messenger sent on the
gravest of business.

Sackville Lane on my right, a revolver on the stones, a hat beside
it. I know that hat. The O'Rahilly, our Director in Arms. Did he
drop it as he ran? Oh Christ save us, that's him, the O'Rahilly,
his feet on a doorstep, his bare head on the curb, still, quite still.

She controls her feelings and walks on.

A shout of command from the ramshackle barricade. That
accent. A beckoning hand. I go up so close, the carved lion-foot
of a table pokes me in the side. 'The Commandant of the Irish
Republican Army wishes to treat with the Commandant of the
British Forces in Ireland.'

(Cockney accent) 'Treat us to what, cream buns?'

'I must speak with the Officer in Charge.'

(Educated English accent) 'You're from the Sinn Féiners?'

'The Irish Republican Army, they call themselves.' They, why did I say they instead of we, was it tact or just cowardice?

A hole opens and they pull me through.

(Cockney) 'How many of you girls are there down there?'

'Three.' Thinking of Winnie, thinking of Sheila, my best pal since we first went to the nuns. Just three out of the forty of us from Cumann na mBan, because the rest were evacuated on Thursday.

(Educated) 'My advice is, go back down, bring the other girls out of there.'

I have to make them listen to me or more hours will be wasted and more of us will be slaughtered. 'The Commandant of the Irish Republican Army wishes to treat with the Commandant of the British Forces.'

(Educated) 'Search her, she's a spy.'

'Not here in the street!'

(Cockney) 'Oh, you'd have us treat you like a lady now?'

That fellow takes me into the National Bank, of all places, and rips off my red crosses. In my apron he finds cakes and sweets, for our men, and two pairs of scissors, and my rosary beads, which he looks at as if they're some class of weapon.

She takes a page out of her apron.

I spend half the afternoon running back and forth along Moore Street, carrying warnings and ultimata, all for the sake of this: the surrender.

She reads aloud.

'In order to prevent the further slaughter of Dublin Citizens and in the hope of saving the lives of our followers now surrounded and hopelessly outnumbered, the members of the Provisional Government present at Headquarters have agreed to an unconditional surrender and Commandants of the various districts in the City and Country will order their Commands to lay down arms. P. H. Pearse, 29th April 3.45pm.'

She puts it back in her apron.

After he has finally handed over his sword, his pistol, his bullets, his canteen, even the two onions in his pockets, I think: it's over.

But I'm mistaken. The British General says, who better than the girl despatcher to bring Pearse's Order of Surrender around to each of the rebel outposts?

The Captain offers to escort me to Stephen's Green in the motorcar. Me, a docker's daughter, gliding along in a motor. 'I might as well show you the sights,' he quips, and he turns down Sackville Street, or what used to be Sackville Street.

Tyler's, where I got these boots; the DBC, where I had potato soup last week, gone. My face doesn't show a thing, if the Captain's looking. Smouldering wreckage, and what's left is banjaxed. But Nelson's pompous Pillar is still standing, lording it over poor Dublin. What have they done, with their artillery batteries and their gunships? What have we all done?

Grafton Street, the windows of jewellers' smashed in. The Captain stops halfway down and tells me it's not safe for him to go any farther. I hoist my stick with its grubby white flag. I walk as far as the Green, where the grass is scarred with fresh-dug trenches. I look down at the Shelbourne Hotel, fourth-floor windows bristling with machine guns. I turn right.

Bullet!

She cringes, then straightens up.

Not mine, not this time.
The grand facade of the College of Surgeons has bits chipped

out of it, confetti of white stone. I go around to the side and knock. Commandant Mallon's sleeping, they tell me, but the Countess comes down in her uniform, and her face lights up because it was her who trained us to shoot, myself and Sheila and Winnie. 'Elizabeth, you're all right?' she asks. And how can I tell her that it's time to give in, give up, give over all our grand schemes?

Later, with the help of a priest, going a roundabout way along the Quays, I find our men in the Four Courts. Commandant Daly is very cut up, but accepts the order, as a soldier.

Later, I track down Commandant MacDonagh at Jacob's Biscuit Factory. His Volunteers insist on blindfolding me before they bring me to him, in case I'm spying for the enemy. How long it takes, how complicated it is, to end a war, even a six-day one.

And all night, in my dreams, for years, I'll still walk these penitential stations, losing myself, explaining myself, crisscrossing Dublin from outpost to outpost. Trying to end it sooner rather than later. Begging good men to stand down with honour before the British hunt them down like rats. As they line up to be arrested, some of them entrust their savings to me to send to their mammies.

The worst is Boland's Mill. I walk all the way from the river to the Grand Canal, jerking my flag, but no sign of any Volunteers.

How can I persuade them to surrender if I can't even find them? Past Holles Street Hospital where I'm supposed to be right now, learning Care of Mothers Before, During and After Birth. Boland's is a labyrinth: the Mill, the Bakery, the Gasworks, the Distillery, old grey walls staring me down. Two loaves of bread on the ground and another bloodstained hat, a woman's this time. I try one door, then another. 'Commandant de Valera?'

Around into Harmony Row, under the railway bridge in Brunswick Place. 'Commandant de Valera!'

Crossing the Grand Canal Street Bridge, an old man wheezing along behind me. A second later I hear a groan and spin around and he's down on his face, blood pooling, because he's caught a bullet meant for me. I scream, then, not like a trained nurse or half-trained even, I scream like a child, I scream at the people who are shut up in their houses, waiting for this week's nightmare to be over, 'Open up for the love of God and take this man in!'

At last on Barrow Street I find some Volunteers, who tell me de Valera's in the Dispensary on Denzill Street that I passed half an hour ago.

When I clamber through that barricade, they send me around to a little window, have me stand on a crate. They lift me in like a parcel.

De Valera, with a towel around his neck, shaving himself.
'You must surrender.' His eyebrows go up. There are none of
us girls serving under de Valera, he wouldn't take us as a gift.
I show him Pearse's note, but he'll have none of it. 'This is a
hoax,' he says, 'to undermine our Insurrection when it's on the
very brink of triumph!'

And I can't tell if the man believes what he's saying, when the
whole city reeks of defeat.

One more thing. The picture. The moment Pearse has handed
over his sword, his pistol, and his onions, the General says,
'A commemorative photograph would be in order, I believe.'
I'm edging away when the photographer crooks his finger.
So I take up my position on the far side of my Commandant.
Not to be seen, at the moment of humiliation. Not to give the
enemy the satisfaction. The junior officer lights a cigarette, for
scorn. 'Hold steady, please,' the photographer calls. And I sway
backwards so the picture won't include me, or only my boots.

Why should I be remembered? All I did was walk through the
ruins. As I still walk in my dreams, all these decades later, with
stiffer legs and flatter feet. None of the bullets were mine, in the
end. What did I do, that I have to live so long, men's faces blurred
in my head, but the smell of blood still fresh? The weight of
memory, like a gravestone over my head.

PADRAIG PEARSE

SIGNATORIES

THOMAS KILROY

PADRAIG PEARSE

BY

THOMAS KILROY

Pearse in his cell before execution. He is thirty-six years old, dressed in the full uniform of the Commander of the Irish Volunteers. He is seated on a chair by a table. On the table are papers, writing material, a blindfold and a crucifix. He may move about but his essential position is a seated one.

I don't like you, Pearse. You know that? Never have. My pathetic otherness, my weakling half. Even when I was a child. I was always trying to get away from you. How could I get away from myself? What an absurdity! We're Siamese twins stuck together. Does everyone have a failed weakling like that inside him? That has to be – eliminated? Actually, I don't think that anyone likes you. I watch their faces as they turn away from you. That look of – distaste. Get me away from this – creature!

What time is it? Taken away my watch. That is the most cruel thing of all. No time. No light. No dawn. Such silence. After all that noise. The sheer noise of that bombardment, deafening. Such a silence now. All stilled.

No. Never liked you. Never! Change that. That's the wrong word, liked! I hate you, Pearse! Hate! Hate! Namby pamby, weakling, no spunk, pasty-faced, pudgy slob, dribbling drawers, afraid of your own shadow – but I am rising above you, you hear – I will leave you behind me as I prepare – prepare myself for the final heroic – that's what's so interesting. It's all so simple. Cleansed myself of all weakness. Just like that. Passed through the flame of purification. I'm ready now.

Always trying to hide, you were, hiding behind Mother's skirts. Not any more. No more hiding. Father was right. He had your measure, my friend, saw through you, he did, saw you for what you were. Wonder what he would think now? I mean think of me? Wonder what he would say about me?

My father the Englishman. What an irony! That self-taught pedant. Don't believe he read half of those books that he had on his shelves.

Willie and I clung to one another in the school-yard on Westland Row while they yelled at us. *(Calling in a sing-song voice)* 'Are you English, Pearse? You sound bloody English! Listen to that accent, boys! Go back to where you came from, Pearse. Back to England.' But we're not in the school-yard now, are we? No. We're somewhere else now. Somewhere beyond geography.

Father used to come up from downstairs, up from below. First the sound. He was on the move! In the studio. Behind the shop. The shuffling sound. Far below us. Then the heavy footsteps – clump! clump! – on the stairs. I knew each board on that stairs that creaked. One, two, and a pause before the third. Creak! I waited for him to step on each board – creak! creak! Then on again. He always stopped before opening the door. As if he were taking a deep breath. When he opened the door we were all pent in silence, Mother and the four of us children, as if stricken.

The huge figure, shrouded in the white dust of the chiselled stone. The giant risen from his den. The stone mason. His hammer and chisel put aside, his apron off. Many times he said nothing at all, just sinking into a chair while Mother prepared the food. And the four of us watched him. Then he would sigh, a sound louder than any one of us could make, a great emission of air, diminishing at the end.

But other times he would grasp us four children. Holding us close, close to his chest, a tumble, close, close. As if trying to convince himself that we still existed.

Didn't like that bit, never liked that part. I was frightened by it, yes, I admit it, frightened of him. He often hurt me with his clasp, although I knew he didn't mean to. I tried to hold back. 'Come here, boy! Come closer!' The rough serge cutting my face. 'Give me your hand, boy! Tight! Tighter! Like this!' Then the whispering. Stubble on the chin, rasping against my cheek, the whispers: 'Is our Pat a Molly boy? Is he? Ha? How are we going to make a man of him, our Paddy? What are we going to do with him? Hah? Stand up straight, boy! Shoulders back!'

When they come for me I will walk out of here. Whistling. Cannot get that boy out of my head, boy in the GPO. And what happened to him. Three o'clock they will come for me. The hour of Golgotha. Sweet Jesus Christ! Christ be my mentor at this hour! Christ be my example in this as in all things. Upon the cross, bruised flesh. Blood. What would he say about me now, if he were here? That's the question. My father, the crude Englishman? Mother at the foot of the cross. Mother, waiting for me to die.

They dragged the boy to me in the GPO. Not to Connolly. To me. It was Wednesday afternoon. Connolly lay on the stretcher beside one of the counters, the usual group around him, the acolytes, the comrades. They were always in attendance, all listening to what he had to say. But the boy was brought to me, dragged across the Main Hall. Not to Connolly, mark you! I can see him still. He had a shock of fair hair across his forehead. He could not have been more than twenty, maybe younger.

At first I yelled at them. 'What is this?' I cried, 'I'm extremely busy, can't you see!' I had been preoccupied all morning trying to put the finishing touches to my manifesto. The noise was tremendous, the bombardment of the heavy guns overhead, the constant small arms fire. I was trying to put what shape I could to the words on the page. 'I must get this out,' I yelled, waving my papers at them. 'This is for posterity!'

They told me that the boy was trying to run away. I saw the fine down on his cheek and the rivulets of sweat on his skin. 'No, sir!' he shouted. 'No, sir! 'Tisn't that at all, so it's not. Not running away.' 'Do you know the penalty for desertion?' I asked him. 'Not a deserter, General, so I'm not.' And I believed him.

I told them to release him. They were still hanging from his arms and shoulders. 'I just want to live, General, so's I can fight in the future,' he explained with that open, innocent face of his. 'Somebody has to go on living. For to fight again. I'm not afraid to die for Ireland, General, so I'm not.'

I hardly listened to him. I was trying to think of the wording of my manifesto. I had to get this right. My final tribute to the men would have to strike precisely the right note. Triumph in the moment of defeat. The record would have to be correct. Written down. Nothing has ever happened until it is written down.

'No one can leave now,' I told the boy. 'The enemy has cut all our lines of communication. Our despatch riders can no longer get through even to North King Street.' Connolly was explaining something to the men around him. They leaned in, to listen. 'The cordon is getting tighter by the hour,' I said to the boy. Why were they always gathered round him like that? 'Headquarters is now isolated,' I announced to the boy. I sounded a trifle pompous, I know, but I felt as if I were making the announcement to the whole world.

The boy shook his head. 'That's all right, General,' he said. 'I'll take me chances. If they get me, they get me. If they don't I'll live to fight another day.'

I brought him out the back. Near to where the men were

tunnelling into Henry Street. Compared to the front of the
Post Office the back was a place of silence. Silence and menace.
Despatch cyclists under their caps were hiding in doorways but
going nowhere. The laneway was empty.

I pointed. 'There's a machine-gun emplacement, down there,'
I told the boy. 'About a hundred and fifty yards.' He flexed like
an athlete about to run a race and my heart beat, painfully. He
was exercising his arms and legs and I had this tremendous need
to protect his body but I could not move. 'I'll take me chances,'
he said again. 'It's the only way to reach Ned Daly's unit,' I
explained to the boy, 'in the Four Courts.' 'Right so, General,'
he said, 'I'm off so!' A boy about to deliver his message.

As God is my witness at first I didn't want him to go! No! But
equally I knew he had to. Then I wanted him to run, to run,
just run! I was now indifferent to the consequences. I would
not allow myself to think of what was waiting for him.

He ran. He zig-zagged from side to side of the laneway in that
perfect silence. He had gone at least a quarter of the way down
before the gun opened up. The sides of the lane threw back
the rat-tat-tat. Somewhere in the dim past an old man stood
in a Grecian field, holding the wreath of olive in his hands
to reward the victor. All that mattered now was to reach the
finishing line, to break the tape, chest out, hands up, all go
to the very end, the final gasp of breath. He was like a white

light just before it was extinguished. He was perfection just a moment before he ceased to be.

What is important now is that I be understood. My manifesto! Where is it?

He searches his pockets, bits of paper and he finds it.

Here it is! They must read it. Even as they are crushed they must read these words!

(Reading) Let me who has led them into this, speak, in my own and my fellow commanders' names, and in the name of Ireland, present and to come, their praise, and ask those who come after them to remember them. If they do not win they will at least have deserved to win. But win it they will although they win it in death.

The distant sound, barely audible, of orders shouted out and of marching feet on a stone floor. 'Left, right! Left, right! Left, right! Halt! Present arms!'

I should have said more to the boy. I should have said to him that we are not alone. This is a glorious time for Europe, I should have said, when the old, shameful earth is restored to clean life through the blood of battle. I know what Connolly would say to all that. Blithering idiocy, that's what he would say. Not one of us, Connolly. No! He's a materialist, Connolly. No spirituality.

The sound of orders and marching feet, now much closer: 'Left, right! Left, right! Halt! At ease!' Pearse listens intently. He rises, facing audience, with the blindfold in his hands.

My father is moving once more down below. I can hear his heavy footsteps on the stairs. He has made me what I am, this big, blundering, innocent Englishman. He has moulded me with those thick fingers of his as if I were putty. He has shaped me into the image of the Angel of Death. I am the messenger, the harbinger of the future. I am no longer matter. My useless body has melted away. I am now air and light.

He whistles a few bars of a 1798 ballad – puts on the blindfold and ties it. Orders ring out once more and Pearse stops whistling, listening: 'Present arms! Aim!' (Pause) 'As you were!' He gropes for the crucifix and holds it with both hands, aloft.

The young man is crouched at the starting line once more, about to run his race. Yet again! And again! And again!

'Present arms!'

As he crouches on the line I brush against his tense, white body as it springs into release.

'*Aim!*'

And I whisper into the shell of his ear. 'Run,' I tell him. *(Fiercely)* 'Run! Run!'

'*Fire!*'

JAMES CONNOLLY

SIGNATORIES

HUGO HAMILTON

JAMES CONNOLLY

BY

HUGO HAMILTON

Lights up. A young woman is slumped in a chair, hair falling down over her face. She raises her head and stands up. She speaks with an Irish accent. There is no background sound, no props apart from the chair.

There was this song she sang. For James Connolly. She talked to us about the Rising that took place in Dublin. She sang a song to us – for James Connolly.

I have a clear memory of this happening.

In England. In Birmingham.

The back door is open. The garden door, that is, onto the street has been left open. I'm standing outside on the pavement and there's a woman leading my little sister away by the hand. The woman is wearing a red coat and she's taking Theresa away, getting her into a car. There's a man in the driving seat with a cigarette in his mouth, his elbow is leaning out the window.

My other sister, Anne, was already in the back seat of the car, that's how I remember it. She had a liquorice shoelace. Her legs were swinging.

Anne was three, and Theresa was two. I was five.

Angela was the baby sitter. She came running out of the house and started pulling Theresa back out of the car. The woman in the red coat was pulling her one way and Angela was pulling her the other way. Her blond curls were bouncing.

We were born in England, but we were Irish.

And Angela. She was Irish. She was from Dublin and she loved James Connolly.

Angela was mad about James Connolly.

Whenever people came to the house, Angela would be asked to sing a song. 'Come on, Angela, give us a song,' and she would stand up and start clearing away the dishes – 'I can't sing, my voice, what song?' My mother would say, 'Angela, for God's sake, leave the dishes alone,' so then Angela would sit back down again and sing the song.

It was her song.

Angela's song.

She wasn't married, Angela. I don't think she ever got married, not to my knowledge. She was in love with James Connolly. And to her, love was something that only came once, it was not something you could repeat over and over again.

For Angela, it was that intense.

Nobody came close to James Connolly.

He was the man she loved. He was already married, with children. He was dead long before Angela was born, in fact. He had been executed, for taking part in the 1916 Rising. He was injured so badly, he couldn't stand up, they had to execute him in a chair, strapped to a chair.

James Connolly.

Angela said he was good at organising a protest. This was long before protesting was a thing that people did. He got a big crowd of people one day to march behind a black coffin with the words 'British Empire' written on the side. Then he threw the coffin into the Liffey and he was arrested.

It was Maud Gonne who got him out. She was the most beautiful woman in Ireland at the time and she got him out of jail, she bought him breakfast.

Which he badly needed, with six children he was always broke.

Angela said James Connolly rescued Ireland.

This is what I remember.

Angela was pulling my sister back out of the car. The woman

in the red coat was pulling her the other way. I was there. I was looking. There was an almighty tug of war, I thought they were going to tear the arms out of her body, Theresa, she was going to be like a doll with no arms, only the sockets.

And the whole thing was happening in silence, that's my memory – no sound, no shouting.

Only the scream.

Theresa gave out a big scream.

Everyone stopped moving. Angela stopped pulling. The woman trying to get Theresa into the car stopped pulling. And the scream kept going all over the street.

And James Connolly.

Angela said there was something that bothered him.

Apart from inequality.

Apart from capitalism and inequality and injustice, and God was never much of a socialist, and the ordinary people of Ireland never getting their fair share of things, and women still being the slaves of slaves.

What bothered James Connolly was this.

It was something they brought up at his court martial. After the Rising was put down and he was arrested and brought before a military tribunal, on a stretcher.

They accused him of being inhumane. 'Imagine that,' Angela said. They were about to execute him in a chair, even though he was going to die of injuries anyhow. And they accused him of wanton cruelty. They said he had taken part in wanton cruelty.

They said he had ordered the detention of a British officer who happened to be inside the GPO on private business, buying a stamp, let's say, when the revolution broke out. They said James Connolly ordered him to be tied up with telephone wire and placed in a telephone box.

He felt badly about that.

The British officer in question, in his testimony, said he was held in the telephone box for hours, he was about to suffocate until one of the men pleaded on his behalf, and James Connolly said – 'I don't care a damn what you do with him.'

I don't care a damn what you do with him.

That makes him look cold-hearted. Like, he was giving his men the signal to do their worst. Whereas, in fact, the British officer was let out of the telephone box and kept in a different place, where he was more comfortable. He survived unharmed.

That got to James Connolly, being remembered as an angry man.

Which he was, let's face it. That was his character. He was angry, he had a sharp tongue, he was argumentative and rude. He was in the habit of objecting to things, making speeches, shouting people down, and so on. He had every right to be angry. He was angry for the working people, for people living in slums, for his parents who escaped the Irish famine.

Everybody must have heard the scream.

My sister Theresa was screaming. My sister Anne was screaming inside the car. And I screamed as well, I'm sure I did.

Three sisters, screaming.

The woman in the red coat let go.

She let go and ran around to get into the front passenger seat, beside the man who was driving. He threw his cigarette butt into the road and drove away. Angela reached in and pulled Anne out of the car at the very last minute, just before the car moved off, with the back door still open.

That's how I remember it.

There was a sound of the tyres screaming.

Maybe it was us screaming, I can't be totally sure.

Tyres screaming and us screaming like tyres screaming.

It took place in Birmingham.

And this is what Angela told us afterwards. She told us the
story of James Connolly, so we would forget. She promised to
teach us the words of the song so we wouldn't remember what
happened, or what didn't happen.

Before James Connolly was taken away to his execution, his
wife was allowed to see him. She was crying and he told her
to stop. He spoke with a Scottish accent, he came from a place
near Edinburgh but he was Irish. He had a stammer, he thought
he would never be Irish enough.

'Lillie, stop,' he said to his wife, 'you'll unman me.'

He was forty-four years of age when they executed him and he
said it as a good way to go.

Angela brought us upstairs.

The night we were rescued from being taken away by strangers, after we were safe again, she got us into the bath to make us forget what happened.

Then she taught us the song.

Three sisters in the bath together, all pink from the hot water.

And Angela–

Singing her song for James Connolly.

She stands holding the back of the chair and sings out.

> A working class hero is something to be.
> A working class hero is something to be.
>
> There's room at the top, they are telling you still.
> But first you must learn how to smile as you kill.
> If you want to be like the folks on the hill.
>
> A working class hero is something to be.
> A working class hero is something to be.
>
> If you want to be a hero then just follow me.
> If you want to be a hero then just follow me.

ÉAMONN CEANNT

SIGNATORIES

FRANK McGUINNESS

ÉAMONN CEANNT

'WAGED'

BY

FRANK McGUINNESS

This is a cell.

There is a table and, if required, a chair.

Éamonn Ceannt is dressed in a soldier's uniform, bloodied.

A distant strain of music from the uilleann pipes.
Éamonn listens and lets it fade.

It's time to pay the piper, as they say. Which coin shall I use?
Should it be those that I first earned playing? A shining sixpence?
A bright shilling? Why can't I recall? What is happening to me?
Did I ever think I would not remember the exact sum? Did it
not seem, once upon a time, a vast fortune, my first pay packet?

He counts out onto the table a few coins, neatly piling them.
These coins may be of his time, or of our time.
They may be a mixture of both.

I was – I am always and ever ready to believe – to maintain my
country is champion of the world, even at games of chance.
Toss a coin.

He does so, catching it.

Heads come up, Ireland wins the day. But hold back – what is this?

He points to the coin.

The imprint of a face, a king's face, the face of England's king –
better settle for tails.

He tosses the same coin.

What matter which side's top? It's all the same. Ireland, every time. Even if that's cheating. Yet I was never a cheat, no man can say different.

He tosses the coin again.

Heads, tails, whatever. Saved, damned, whatever.

He adds the coin to the pile.

I have been gambling with my soul. What I have done – is it sinful? Has it sent me to perdition?

From his pocket he takes out another coin.
He adds it to the pile.

I have killed another man. Another soldier. I have killed him in war. That is what soldiers do. It is what they are paid for. In pounds, shillings and pence.

From his pocket he takes out another coin.
He adds it to the pile.

The wages of war. So I did to him as he would have done to me. Should I have whispered in his ear as he died an act of contrition? I am grievously sorry I have offended in word, act or thought, and I resolve never again – never – have I sent him to hell? Or is he in paradise?

He takes out another coin.

Heads or tails?

He tosses the coin, lets it fall, does not pick it up.

Who am I to say? Who am I to tell? Who does he leave behind him? A wife?

He adds another coin to the pile.

A father?

He adds another coin to the pile.

A child?

He adds another coin to the pile.

When they received the news, what did they cry through Birmingham – husband? Or did they weep in Glasgow – father? Through the streets of Cardiff, did his mother keen – son? Who am I to say?

The beat of a drum.

He sits.

From his pocket he takes out a gold watch on a silver chain.
He moves it slowly to and fro before his eyes.
He sings lowly to himself.

> Who stole my watch and chain, watch and chain, watch
> and chain, who stole my watch and chain—

He stops singing as the watch continues to move to and fro.

My worldly goods – these coins, this watch and chain. They
were about my person when I fought against the odds, almighty
odds, Herculean odds, for my poor country against the might
of empire, brilliantly equipped with weapons and with men,
and I sent one such man from this green earth to his repose
where he now lies in his grave, his bed of ebony – or is this a
white dream, from which we will wake, stare at each other's
eyes, and see that we both sleep, enchanted by time, passing
time, a watch and chain, held in the hand of a god playing with
our souls, gambling with our souls, wondering what we've
done? Are we sent to perdition?

He sings.

> Who stole my watch and chain, watch and chain, watch
> and chain, who stole my watch and chain—

Silence.

He stops moving the watch and chain to and fro.
He looks about him.

This cell, what is it?

He holds the watch to his right ear.
He points to the watch.

This tells me it is my country. What does my country ask of me?

He holds the watch to his left ear.
He points to the watch.

This tells me to kill for it. And if I kill for it, would I die for it?

Silence.

How should I die for it?

He winds the silver watch chain about his clenched fist.
He raises the fist, displaying the watch face.

It tells me the time – time to die. It is near, death. And what is it? A smell of fear. A touch of bone. A taste of fire. A sound of nothing. A hood of sight. A broken mirror. A shard of fear, a piece of bone, a blood of fire, a crack of nothing, a sliver of sight.

He unwinds the chain from round his fist.
He places it and the watch beside the mound of coins.
From his pocket he takes a set of black rosary beads.
He sings.

Hail Queen of Heaven, the—

Silence.
He sings.

Remind thy Son that he—

Silence.
He sings.

The price of our iniquity.

Silence.
He sings.

Pray for the—

Silence, as he starts to finger the rosary beads.

Shall I say my rosary? Recite the mysteries, joyful, glorious,
steeped in sorrow? Shall these beads be my armour, deflecting
the bullets my enemies fire against me? Shall they keep me safe

this day and the days to come as they have until now? Or is their work over and I must face the salvo alone, unaided, asking no favour but the strength to die as a soldier? Shall I leave them beside the rest of all I own, for now who can hear me?

Silence, as he stops fingering the beads.

He can hear, the man I shot. How does he answer me? With what voice does he speak? Is it my own? What does he say? What does he call me?

Silence.

Father?

Silence.

Husband?

Silence.

Child?

Silence.

Child, beloved child, whose voice is to me – the playing of the pipes, the beating of soft drums, the shiniest of sixpences,

the best of all wages, my finest of first pays, my champion, my
country – forgive me.

Silence.

Child, forgive your father.

Silence.

For dying, forgive me. For living. Doing what was done,
forgive me. Doing what was needed. What can I leave you
to remember me, Éamonn Ceannt? Only these. A watch.
A chain. A rosary. A few shillings.

He points to the pile of coins, the watch, the chain, the beads.

One thing – one thing more.

From his pocket he takes out a worn latchkey.
He kisses it.
He breathes on it as if it is his last breath.

The greatest treasure I possessed.

He holds the key in his open palms.
There is the beat of a drum.

The key to my home.

Several beats of the drum.

The address is 13, Alphonsus Road, Drumcondra.

Silence.
A gentle drumbeat.

Drumcondra, Dublin.

Silence.
A gentle drumbeat.

Ireland.

A gentle drumbeat.
Silence.
The music of the uilleann pipes plays.
Darkness.

THOMAS CLARKE

SIGNATORIES

RACHEL FEHILY

THOMAS CLARKE

BY

RACHEL FEHILY

Clarke is alone in his cell in Kilmainham Gaol. It is the 3rd of May 1916, 3.30am, he will be executed at 4.30am that morning. His arm is injured and in a sling. There is a chair with a table in front of it in the centre of the stage facing the audience. The set is lit by candlelight. He is singing 'A Nation Once Again' to himself to keep up his spirits.

> When boyhood's fire was in my blood
> I read of ancient freemen,
> For Greece and Rome who bravely stood,
> Three hundred men and three men–

We've done it, I knew the lads would do it. They came out and fought the fight. And oh, what a glorious fight it was!

I had the finest men and women in the land at my side, I shot the lock on the GPO and Connolly, Mac Dermott, Plunkett and Pearse fell back a step to let me enter first – they called me their president.

Every second of every day of the fifteen years I spent in gaol in England was worth it for that one magnificent moment.

> And then I prayed I yet might see
> Our fetters rent in twain,
> And Ireland, long a province, be
> A Nation once again!

The sun shone on us while they reduced the city to rubble, despite our numbers we held firm. I would rather have died in battle – but there is some decency in this ending. And the end of all of us will be no ending for the English. It will be Ireland's beginning.

They will pay dearly, their every murder will be returned to them hundreds of times.

It is our good fortune that the English will never learn the simple lesson that each time they trample other nations with their presumptuous greed and ignorant force, feign surprise at the resistance of idealists and attempt to suppress them with murder; that they gain nothing. They are igniting the long fuses of the dynamite, that is bound to explode in their witless faces.

> A Nation once again,
> A Nation once again,
> And Ireland, long a province, be
> A Nation once again!

No doubt you'll see reams of bad as well as good in the months to come, written about what's happened in all the papers. I trust you to have the sense to decide upon your own opinions and not to have your fine minds influenced by the rubbish written by damned fool journalists and historians, saboteurs who are of a vindictive bent or idiots who know no better.

Presently it will come to be widely known that the Germans were true to their promises and MacNeill was nothing but a weak traitor. Time will correct the mistakes that were made but those whom we all know were treacherous poltroons will never be forgiven and have no part in our future.

An old woman in a fine black dress and feathered hat spat at us in the streets as they marched us up Henry Street to the Rotunda:

'May you burn in hell for killing innocent little children!'

If I believed in their God I might believe that I will burn in hell, for my actions did cause death to others. But that blood is on English hands, for their sins the few must suffer for the many.

The war to free the whole island will be short and savage. Brothers who fall out with each other are more ferocious than animals and you will experience deadly, turbulent times, but so long as you hold strong, never say die, and be ready and willing to give it your all, within your time Ireland will finally be able to take its place, head held high, among all nations, peacefully and prosperously.

As soon as it's over we'll live together in a magnificent new united Ireland where men and women work side by side bonded by virtuous ideals, our citizens exist together in harmony, all are valued equally whatever their religion and the strong look after the weak.

You will see no more barbarism of the sort that I had the misfortune to see when I was a boy, because our noble patriots have a natural kindness and will never treat anyone on our island whether Irish or a foreign guest, the way the English treated us, subjecting our people to humiliation, prison and torture, starving and exiling our forefathers for the 'crime' of seeking freedom.

> So as I grew from boy to man,
> I bent me to that bidding
> My spirit of each selfish plan
> And cruel passion ridding;
> For thus I hoped one day to aid,
> Oh can such hope be vain?
> When my dear country shall be made—

I did not make a confession, but I confess to you that it grieves me to wait here for my death like a sick patient. I know my time has come and yet I am well. Well enough to ponder, yet nothing else. I am left alone with my reflections, well enough. I am ready.

I confess to you that it troubles me that I picked such a hard road for our family and I am stricken that my three little boys are unfairly sentenced to a life without their father and no hope of amnesty.

Circumstances dictated that this was the only way.

We have no need of priests to comfort us or teach us wrong

from right. They have not stood up for our people as they should have. I believe that God and our own courage will help my children bear the loss. Their mother will tell them that I have no fear to finally go and stand before a real judge who will recognise a patriot's sacrifice for the greater good.

I cannot tell you the comfort I feel knowing that I leave the future of our struggle safely in her hands. Hands that can hold a gun better than many men. She is afraid of nothing. Watch her, for she will fan the flames that we have lit into a roaring fire. I am full of pride for her – my finest soldier.

Last night they gave me a choice, pen and paper to write to my Katty, or they would send for her to visit me.

I had no choice but to see her. For I fear and believe that I will never see her again.

It wasn't that I didn't want to say goodbye. We knew when I went out that it was the end for us. I count myself fortunate to have spent my life with a woman for whom my affection is so deep that I could not bring myself to say goodbye. Some things cannot be said.

The look on her face when she came into the cell. It troubled me.

'Why did you surrender? The last thing you said, Tom, was no surrender.'

I told her it was not my decision and I would have preferred to die in battle.

'You will go to your death undaunted for you have saved the soul of Ireland. You have struck the first successful blow for freedom and that freedom is coming, but between now and freedom Ireland will go through hell but we will never lie down again.'

I swore to her I needed no blindfold to face them.

'Don't be afraid, Tom, be strong for our children and be happy for us all and for Ireland. Think of the future.'

I said nothing. Oh I wanted to take her in my arms, to hold her and be next to her in this stinking cell but I did not. To do so in this place...

It was not what I wanted.

And it was not what she wanted.

I saw on her face that there was no longer any soft tenderness for me, there was something new – something frightening.

I fancied that I no longer existed. I not her husband, nor father to our children.

I was Tom Clarke. A leader of the Rising. A signatory of the Proclamation, the author of my own death warrant.

It was all over between us.

My Katty looked at me with a different love on her face and I know it was not a love for me. It was a stronger love. A higher sacred love, a love of our country, our struggle and our dreams.

And that is as it should be for we were one and the same, what brought us together is parting us. I am gone but she still has her love. She said it to me didn't she? That I went out to save the soul of Ireland. Not my own soul.

Did we love each other enough? Or did we both love Ireland more? I wanted to be a man, her man, for our last moments together but did I ever belong to anyone or anything except this damned struggle?

> It whispered too that freedom's ark
> And service high and holy,
> Would be profaned by feelings dark
> By passions vain or lowly;
> For freedom comes from God's right hand
> And needs a Godly train
> And righteous men must make our land–

I know your secret Katty.

I wanted to tell you before you left that I knew, the secret you couldn't tell me.

Of late she is with child and she did not say it because she feared it would undo me. She worried that it might sway me to speak of her future confinement. She was concerned that it might have affected my ability to go out on Easter Sunday. My judgment. She did not want to affect my judgment.

She did it to help me. She was right not to tell me. She feared that I could not face the guns this morning with sufficient courage if 'twas ever mentioned. She put Ireland before everything.

It was for the best. We had no need to speak of our unborn child. Other things are more important. If we put ourselves first nothing can ever be achieved.

> And from that time, through wildest woe
> That hope has shone a far light,
> Nor could love's brightest summer glow
> Outshine that solemn starlight;
> It seemed to watch above my head,
> In forum, field, and fane,
> Its angel voices sang round my head–

'What happens when we die, Papa?'

'I will not be gone boys, I will always be there watching over you. See up there in the sky, among the stars with all the other souls.'

'I will always be there for you just like the moon.'

It is my regret that I worked too hard and I fear that I did not spend sufficient time with my children. Their sweet good natures sustained me through difficult days. I could never be angry for long with thoughts of their smiling faces constantly in my head.

I did not say goodbye to Daly and Tom.

'Daddy, will you play soldiers with us one last time?'

I set up a fine battle for them to play with. I kissed their curls and tickled them until they howled at me to leave them alone and then I walked away.

Little Emmet, he's no more than a baby.

'Am I too old to sleep in your bed?' he asked.

'It's time to grow up, little man,' I told him. Katty will be lonely. I hope he creeps in at night and gives her my hugs and kisses.

I hope they think of me when they look at the moon.

And you — my silent wisp of life so nearly close to me.

You will know nothing of me except the curses or praise that will be heaped upon my memory.

Be sure in your heart forever that it was love, and only love, that caused me to leave you this costly legacy.

No angels will have sweeter faces than you and your brothers-to-be, and I know…

It is a worthy legacy. It is a legacy for the soul of Ireland.

> When boyhood's fire was in my blood
> I read of ancient freemen,
> For Greece and Rome who bravely stood,
> Three hundred men and three men;
> And then I prayed I might yet see
> Our fetters rent in twain
> And Ireland long a province be—

There is no one to pray to. There is nothing left...

> And Ireland long a province, be
> A Nation once again!

SEÁN Mac DIARMADA

SIGNATORIES

ÉILÍS Ní DHUIBHNE

SEÁN MAC DIARMADA

BY

ÉILÍS Ní DHUIBHNE

A cell in Kilmainham. Min Ryan, plump and fair, dressed in dusty pink chiffon, furs, lace.

> I am Brian Boy Magee –
> My father was Eoghain Bán –
> I was wakened from happy dreams
> By the shouts of my startled clan;
> And I saw through the leaping glare
> That marked where our homestead stood,
> My mother swing by her hair –
> And my brothers lie in their blood.

This is where we sat. The three of us. Me, Seán, and Phyllis. My sister. One of my sisters – I have seven. Phyllis said I'd need someone to be with me when I was leaving the jail, and I said, 'yes, yes of course, thank you very much, that's very thoughtful.' Although to tell the truth I hadn't given it a moment's consideration. Leaving, saying goodbye. No. That was one of those ideas, like the word 'dead', that I couldn't imagine. The only thought in my head was about going to see him, to say hello. I knew. But I couldn't imagine him not being alive.

Phil said she'd wait in the entrance hall until I was ready to leave. They gave her a seat; they were polite enough. Of course everyone was polite to Phyllis...

But when I told Seán she was in the hall he insisted she come
and join us.

That was Seán all over. And I didn't mind, really, having her
there. It's not as if we were alone anyway. There was a soldier in
the cell all the time, near the door, God knows why. We were
hardly going to make a run for it. And the poor creature didn't
know where to look. Stood like a statue and stared at the wall.
Not that there was anything to embarrass him.

Pause.

Seán wasn't like Risteard. My fiancé. My husband-to-be.

(Smiles) You know? Seán was shy, is how I would put it. In that
way. But he was my first real boyfriend and I thought this is
how it always is. You meet for coffee or tea or to go to a céilí,
you listen to the man talking about himself, and then, 'Oíche
Mhaith, a Sheáin.' He never kissed me. Not properly. *(Pause)*
He was from Leitrim. *(Pause)* And on this night, the night of
the 11th of May, when I came in he gave me a nice big hug.
Followed by a quick peck on the cheek. And then we were both
lost for words. Most unusual for Seán Mac Diarmada. As chatty
as a magpie he was, usually. I couldn't say what I was thinking,
which was, 'You look terrible. You look like death's door.'

I said, 'Seán, you big amadán! Why didn't you tell me you were going to start the whole shebang on Easter Monday?'

He didn't even tell me there would be a Rising. And I went haring off to Wexford on the train bringing a message telling the Wexford Volunteers the whole thing was cancelled. If he'd been a bit less secretive they wouldn't have got that message and who knows? He mightn't have been sitting here waiting to be shot. We might have ... well, we might have held out for a bit longer anyhow.

He laughed, 'Sorry, a thaisce. We couldn't tell anyone.' He looked at the soldier. 'Tá an tír lofa le spiodóirí.'

I'm your fiancée, for God's sake. I thought. I'm not a spy.

But I said, 'Dhein tú an rud ceart.' The guard let a tiny little frightened squeal out of him. So I switched to French. 'Phil est ici.' 'Sure tell her to come in!' 'But ...' Before I could say another word he gave a nod to the guard and your man nodded back, and vamoosed – Seán would make friends with the devil if he had two minutes with him in a waiting room.

> In the creepy cold of the night
> The pitiless wolves came down –
> Scotch troops from that Castle grim
> Guarding Knockfergus Town
> And they hacked and lashed and hewed

With musket and rope and sword,
Till my murdered kin lay thick
In pools by the Slaughter Ford.

Next thing in bounces the bould Phyllis. She got the hug and peck
on the cheek too. He even helped her to set a hairpin to rights.

Nattered on to beat the band. It was for all the world like
meeting him for a cup of coffee in the DBC. No coffee, of
course. We'd brought in tea in a flask – he didn't like coffee,
much, he wasn't used to it. With his background, you know.
That little farm in the back of beyond. She had some whiskey
and a few cigars. But he didn't bother with anything except the
tea and the cigar.

She wraps her furs around her.

It's always freezing in here. Even in May, it felt cold. He put
his arm around us to keep us warm. He was so excited I don't
think he felt anything.

And what was there to be excited about, you might ask?

'I feel happiness the like of which I have never felt before. I die
so the Irish nation might live.'

'Mon Dieu!' Phyllis gave me such a look. He didn't see the look but he must have felt something because then he patted me on the head.

'I'll miss you, a stór, of course. But we'll meet again, some day, in a better place.'

Pause.

Then he was off again like a hound out of the trap telling us all about the week, things we'd heard a dozen times at that stage. What this one said and what that one said. Who saved someone's life by producing a cup of tea and a cigar at the crucial moment. The endless meetings and discussions and risky decisions. We'd relived it a thousand times. Sure you probably feel the same? But naturally we let him tell his own version. That it was all down to him and poor old Tom. They were the ones who decided it was time to make a stand, and were at the meeting with Pearse on Easter Sunday when they decided definitely to come out on Monday. He told us about going to the GPO, himself and Tom, dressed in their ordinary clothes, ahead of the garrison, and waiting there outside for the Volunteers to arrive. When the place was occupied they just walked in as if they were going to buy a stamp.

And joined them. You know all this, I know, but Seán told the story and now I like telling it too. Over and over again. You're not the first I've told it too, I might as well admit. It's getting

to be my party piece. I suppose I'll stop telling it after I get
married.

He walked from the Rotunda to Richmond Barracks, without
his walking stick. Some officer took it from him. There's always
a nasty type who gets a rise out of being cruel. Seán had to lean
on the shoulders of two men, dragging his poor weak leg, all
the way out to Inchicore. You know he had polio? He didn't
really have the use of his left side, it must have been agony.
That's the part I find hardest to take. Him struggling along for
miles without the stick.

Her voice breaks.

But he made it. And he made himself useful as soon as he
got there. To Richmond Barracks. The place stank to high
heaven because there was just one receptacle. For all of them.
Hundreds in the big room, the old gym, I believe. Yes, well,
anyway, he being himself, being a trade unionist you might say,
hammered on the door until one of the officers came and he
managed to get them to do something about it. Get some class
of a commode.

> I fought by my father's side,
> And when we were fighting sore
> We saw a line of their steel
> With our shrieking women before;

The red-coats drove them on
To the verge of the Gobbins gray,
Hurried them – God! the sight!
As the sea foamed up for its prey.

He told a story about a cigar. How Tom Clarke got a cigar and
how ten of them sat on the floor like schoolboys and passed the
cigar around, one to one, in that stinking place. Waiting to find
out whether they'd live or die. He made it sound like a camping
holiday. Fun with the lads.

But he didn't forget the girls. Not he. After a while says he:
'Do you think my old girlfriends would like something to
remember me by?'

'What?'

'I mean, just some class of a memento.'

'Oh, I'm quite sure your old girlfriends would love that!' Phil
said. 'God, you're a scream, so you are!'

'But what can you give them?' I looked around the cell.

Seán looked around the cell. Even the guard had a look. There
isn't much in it now and there wasn't then either. The only thing
Seán had was the clothes on his back … Yes. Anyway, he took off

his blazer, and started to pull the buttons off. Brass buttons.

'It's all I've got,' he was hard set to pull them off. He was hard set to do it. He'd no scissors needless to say.

'Your legacy to your girlfriends will be buttons?' Phil laughed.

'Would you ever stop. Min, tell her what my legacy will be.'

'Your legacy is a free and Gaelic Ireland, a republic where all the children of the nation will be cherished equally.'

'Exactly ... I die so Ireland can live. A free and happy nation will be my legacy.' He hacked out another one. 'And buttons for the girls. This one is for Sinéad,' he said. 'And Mary can have this one. And here, for Kathleen Clarke. You could maybe cut them in two, girls? There won't be enough to go round.'

'We'll make quarters of them. You write a list for us. Seán Mac Diarmada leaves a quarter of a button to the following female children of the nation ...'

He was never conceited, not more than any other young fellow. Sure nothing would get done if we didn't allow the lads their arrogance, poor things. And it turned out he was perfectly right. All his old friends were delighted to get a button. I suppose anything a person wears — it's a link, isn't it, to their body?

It's funny that buttons last longer than people. Not that buttons have much of a life. And there's a distance about them. Hard little yokes they are.

I have something softer myself. His blue tweed tie.

She takes it out of her bag and twists it around her hand.

I know from some of the others that it was different, in their cells, on the last night. The Connollys. The Clarkes. They weren't laughing, not at all. The Plunketts. They got married. There was no question of that with me and Seán. All he wanted to do that night was to entertain us, to forget about what was about to happen.

We stayed for a long time. Hours, three hours maybe. He never stopped talking. The last thing he did was recite a few verses of his favourite poem.

> I am Brian Boy Magee –
> My father was Eoghain Bán –
> I was wakened from happy dreams
> By the shouts of my startled clan;

He would have recited more if he'd got a chance but then it was time. He hugged me and he hugged Phil and then the priest came into the cell and we said, 'Slán leat, slán leat,' as if we would meet again in a few days' time in Bewley's. That's how it was. That's how it had to be.

It was still dark. As we left the jail one bird started singing in the trees. A gentle rain was falling, but I didn't want to get a cab straight away, I wanted a walk in the morning rain to wash the jail air out of me. I felt impatient, irritated. At that moment I just wanted it all to be over, the whole thing, I wanted to move back into ordinary life where there are no Risings or shootings or court martials or executions.

We walked down towards Islandbridge. The river flows fast there, over the weir, between grassy banks. By then the birds were singing in their hundreds, in the trees in the Park. And there was a finger of pink light in the sky over Kingsbridge.

'Brian Boy Magee,' Phyllis said. 'Could you have married someone who recited that poem at parties?'

We were giddy. We were laughing. I suppose we had had no sleep. That does things to you. Phyllis imitated him, as we walked down Conyngham Road. She's vicious sometimes.

> I am Brian Boy Magee!
> And my creed is a creed of hate;
>
> Love, Peace, I have cast aside –

But Vengeance, Vengeance I wait!
Till I pay back the four-fold debt
For the horrors I witnessed there,
When my brothers moaned in their blood,
And my mother swung by her hair.

My mother swung by her hair?

By then we had reached the river again. And the sun came up
in the east where the Liffey meets the sea and the black water
began to come to life. The air was full of the smell of hops,
sweet and heavy as treacle and seagulls circled in the sky over
the brewery. A heron was standing on a rock in the river on
one leg, like a ballerina. Everything very quiet. Dublin was
dreaming for a moment, that strange time just before you wake
up. Kingsbridge was like Westminster Bridge, in the poem.
All quiet and glittering in the morning air.

And next thing, we heard the shots.

THOMAS MacDONAGH

SIGNATORIES

MARINA CARR

THOMAS MacDONAGH

BY

MARINA CARR

Clarke first, then Pearse, then me. Half past three I'm told. Earlier I asked Aloysius to go and see were they using blindfolds but he hasn't returned yet and it's quarter past now so it's unlikely he will. 'Ah, Tom,' he said, 'ah, Tom,' and took my two hands in his.

I've said my prayers, had the last rites for what they're worth, written to Muriel and the children. I wish to God they'd let me wash. I stink to high heaven, have hardly closed my eyes in a week, my feet, my hands, filthy.

And it's a ridiculous thing to be thinking before you go to your maker but I could do with a good feed, and a glass of wine wouldn't go astray. One of Mam's roast lamb dinners, new spring lamb, done to perfection, Sunday afternoon in Cloughjordan, the whole lot of us around the table digging in, the good tablecloth and the cut glass, my father hung over and mild, carving dreamily as my mother heaps our plates.

Or one of those cheap little bistros I frequented in Paris; I call to mind one in particular on the Rue Mouftard where the workers ate. They'd give you two courses and as much wine as you wanted for a few francs. And the heat, Lord the heat in the smoky little room and I'd sit for hours with my notebooks, over the wine, watching the men and listening to their talk.

And the ladies, swish and glamorous, prancing about as if they were the last word. You have to hand it to them. They'd

convince you that they were Helen of Troy come again until
you put your glasses on and took a good look at the fine Gallic
hooters on the lot of them.

I should've stayed in Paris writing my poems because whichever
way you look at it, this fiasco, this little skirmish of ours, is the
stuff of prose.

At least I wasn't tortured, I don't know about the others.
Aloysius tells me not and I suppose we must be grateful for that.
I thought Englishmen prided themselves on being gentlemen.
And in my experience most of them are, but their treatment of
us since we surrendered has been far from gentlemanly. Herded
in like cattle. No food bar a cup of warm tea and a hard biscuit.
Nowhere to wash yourself or obey the call of nature.

My men were very angry, what with the surrender and
the jeering and booing on the streets as they marched us to
Richmond and the exhaustion and hunger, tempers were up.
Took me a while to calm them down, talk sense to them, let's
show them what real manners are, boys.

Oldest trick in the book, dehumanise the man, starve him, let
him sleep on the wet stones in his clothes, putrid with wear and
dirt, freeze him. By God they have it down to a fine art.

And I'm proud to say my men calmed down, rallied, helped

each other, though some of the younger ones were very afraid, tears in the dark, that sort of thing, shocked, all of us, to find ourselves here, the dream over, for us anyway.

Surely to God they won't kill us all. Line those young fellas up against the wall. Myself, yes. I thought it might be a possibility but I can't say I ever thought it would be like this.

I wonder will they give my body back. Mary, my sister, was here earlier this evening. That's what she wanted to know. 'Will they give us back your body, Tom?' 'I don't know, Mary,' I said, 'but I doubt it.' They're thorough. Centuries of this, and they wouldn't be wanting any shrines made out of this mangy carcass.

I asked her to look after the children because Muriel is not the strongest. She does her best but she's, as the mother would say, highly strung and the nerves do be at her. 'Help her, Mary,' I said, 'don't let them Giffords have their way in the rearing of my children.' Muriel's mother is a handful to say the least. Never really approved of me though I did my best to get on with her. I don't want her around my children. I don't think she will love them in the right way. And I felt a fraud saying that. I who will never love them again. What was I thinking? Certainly not of them. And to top it all I'm leaving them without a penny. I should be at home marking exam papers.

Takes out rosary beads.

Mary gave me these. My mother's rosary beads. I didn't want to take them. 'They'll be shot to pieces,' I said. 'They won't,' she said, 'and I'll get them back later.' And she starts to cry, my sister, the nun, and she takes me in her arms, 'Mam would've wanted you to have them.' And then of course I'm crying, floods, the thought of my beautiful mother and how she worshipped her children. And for the first time I'm glad she's gone to her eternal rest because the thought of what this would do to her is too much to bear.

I don't have much truck with the next world, but if you're there, Mam, come to me now, give me courage to die well. Even the bravest I'm told can lose the run of themselves at the end. Let me keep it together. And if I'm given a choice, which I doubt, but if I am, I'd rather no blindfold. Think I'm more worried about the blindfold than the rest of it.

And God forgive me for saying this but, as a young man and a not so young man – until very recently if truth be told – I thought there was something romantic about death by firing squad. To be shot at dawn, I always thought had a romantic twang to it. Maybe it appealed to the morbid or the gothic in me but I thought it had a certain sort of terrible charm to it.

Of course I forgot to picture myself against the wall with the hands tied behind my back and the blindfold on. And sometimes

they put a piece of white paper over your heart for the squad
to aim at. A lack of imagination you might say because now I
realise there is nothing romantic about the whole caper.

What it will mean for others I will never know but what I feel
right now is that there is nothing great or glorious in finding
yourself about to be taken out between the hours of three and
four in the morning to be shot. In fact I find it ridiculous and
faintly embarrassing and somehow not real, as if it is happening
to someone else.

I read somewhere that between three and four in the morning
we are least on our guard and therefore most open and
susceptible to attack. It can be no accident this is the hour they
have chosen. We've obviously read the same book. No doubt
some flunkey in the war ministry has made a study of it. And
you have to wonder is there any hope for the race at all when
we devise these unnecessary tortures to inflict the maximum
pain on the already vanquished.

And to top it all it's May. It's summer. I'd forgotten that
between the jigs and the reels of these last few weeks. Tom
MacDonagh it's summer and you're a man always enjoyed your
summers. Teaching finished, months of freedom to write, play
your piano, go to the beach, sand between your toes, watch the
children splash in the waves, buckets and spades.

I was going to bring Muriel to Paris this summer with the money from the new book. Show her all my old haunts, parade her up and down the Boule Miche of an evening. She'd buy and sell those French lassies for style and the waist on her and the thick hair. And she hasn't come. I wonder why? It's not like her. Maybe it's too much for her. I know Kathleen has been in to see Tom, and Aloysius told me Agnes has seen Michael. She won't come now.

Sound of key turning.

They're here, the soldiers, two of them. 'Give me one minute,' I say.

Takes photographs from his pocket. Kisses them.

Barbara. Donagh. Muriel. My three loves. My three darlings.

Puts photographs back in his pocket.

'Alright Lads,' I say, 'show me the way.' And I follow them down the dark stinking corridor and then down another passage, the soldiers lighting the way, candles in jam jars, reminds me of going up the stairs to bed at home as a child, my mother ahead of me with the lamp.

In the yard the soldiers stand in a group smoking. They turn
and look at me, hard to see in the flickering light but they seem
nervous, afraid. And young, very young. They don't want to
kill me. One lad blesses himself, sighs. 'It's okay,' I say to him,
'courage, young man, all in a day's work.'

I take out my silver cigarette case, offer them round, some shy
away but some accept and look at me in wonder. I give the
remainder and the case to the officer in charge. 'I won't be
needing it,' I say. 'You're a prince, Mr MacDonagh,' he says and
puts a hand on my shoulder and walks me towards the sandbags.

The hands are tied behind my back and the blindfold goes on
and it's not as bad as I expected and I hear the sounds of the
soldiers lining up and the muffled commands of the officer
and I think they'll probably make some awful myth out of me
and thank God my legs are not shaking and my father flashes
through my mind, him sitting in the parlour nursing his glass,
me and John arguing politics with him and him waving his big
strong hand in dismissal. 'Keep away from them Fenians,' he's
saying, 'just steer clear of them. Great cry, little wool, like the
goats of Connacht.'

JOSEPH MARY PLUNKETT

SIGNATORIES

JOSEPH O'CONNOR

JOSEPH MARY PLUNKETT

'TEN MINUTES'

BY

JOSEPH O'CONNOR

Lights up on a young very frail man, kneeling on a prayer step, head bowed, hands joined.

A few long moments of silence.

As he rises, we see that he is beautifully dressed, having high tan leather boots, spurs, pince-nez.

He slowly paces the space. Takes a fob watch from his waistcoat. Appears to notice the audience.

Occasionally, while speaking, he coughs or becomes short of breath. Sometimes he pulls a grubby bloodstained handkerchief from his elegant pocket to mop his brow or wipe his mouth.

Ten minutes.

Yes.

That's how long they gave us.

A ten-minute marriage.

He laughs softly.

No wonder we were so happy.

The crack of a volley of rifles.

We met – do you know, I can't remember how we met.
She was like a Botticelli made of fire.

Beautiful, elusive, eyes like the sea. Full of truth and that sense that time is slowly passing, that there's nothing we can do but observe it, try to honour it, or believe it – or stay out of its bloody way.

He laughs.

But there was another, you see. My Grace had a rival. Old story, don't you know. No new ones.

My mistress, too, was beautiful and elusive. I had tried to put her away from me – God knows I tried. But she was demanding of everything, my soul, my way of seeing. Once wooed, she would not be dismissed.

You've heard of her, I think.

She's called Ireland.

He takes a drink of water. And spits it out.

Daddy was, among other things, a property developer. I believe you've had your troubles with those, down the years. You'll have heard of Saint Oliver Plunkett, various parts of whom were removed from various other parts by our old friends across the water, Lord bless 'em? Well, Saint Oliver was my ancestor. Which is nice to know. Someone's up there already, putting in a word for me. He lost his head for Ireland. In this, he wasn't alone.

So many have died for Ireland. If only one or two had opted to live for it.

Oh well.

There it is.

The crack of a volley of rifles.

As a child, I was sickly. Found it hard to breathe. The eastern religions preach that grief is stored in the lungs, that loss is actually physical. Talk a lot of rot, but it rather makes one think, no? Grief stored in the lungs. Perhaps.

A sudden and very violent fit of coughing. From which he wills himself to recover.

Which wasn't as bad as you might think, all the same. Because it gave me the chance to read. I loved a book, do you know, as others love a friend. At my public school, in England, the other boys used to mock me. Not easy having the name 'Mary' at a public school in England. *(Chuckles)* I've always loved the English, found them tolerant and kind, reasonable when sober, wildly generous when drunk. At Stonyhurst, I felt wanted. Marvellous people, the English. The upper classes especially. Best of all. They adored Ireland, you see. Really missed having it to play with. Like a dog misses a rat.

The crack of a volley of rifles.

Then came Larkin. Ha! That long streak of Liverpudlian anger. Is there any city on Christ's earth that is *ghastlier* than Liverpool? *(In Scouse accent)* 'The ghreat are only ghreat because we are on our knees, let us arise!' But yet, one couldn't help but feel he was a sort of artist, had a way of seeing.

That Ireland didn't need to be a slum with a casino attached. That the poor are not poor because of bad luck or idleness. The poor are the poor because we must have the poor. Without them, the rest of us couldn't be rich. It's not the natural order. It's a work of fiction.

So on a bright November morning, I attended a meeting. Have you ever smelled poverty? I mean, actually inhaled it? People who reek of their irrelevance and thousand-year belittlement. Who've been told all their lives that their children don't matter? Never did, don't now, never will. Well, a rather strange sort of energy fills a people when this is what they're told. Rather hard to get the genie back in the bottle.

Mummy had taken the lease on Larkfield House in Kimmage *profonde*. Rather posh. Like a manor in Dickens. From early 1914, it became the base, if that's what one would call it, of the 4th battalion, Dublin Brigade, of the Irish Volunteers. If that's what one would call it.

Mummy and the butler would bring them out cocoa when they'd finished their manoeuvres, and cucumber sandwiches, on polished silver salvers. 'Aren't they dashing?' she'd remark. As though speaking of her pets. Which in a way, she was, of course.

Up and down they trudged. Christ help us, the 4th battalion. Boys too young to shave. Withered old men. Virgin old donkey-men with womanly faces. Hungry. In rags. Resentful of being alive. I loved every single one of them. My absolute heroes.

Don't ever dare to criticise those people, not to me.

You had three meals today. They had nothing. But nothing.

And you sleep in silent safety because of what they chose to do for you.

I don't ask you to praise. No, no. That is your choice. I don't even ask for respect. No gentleman would ever dream of asking for that.

But you will not belittle those heroes in my presence. I don't give you the permission you would need.

You may tell me, 'There is no need to address us like this.'

I will answer, 'I am glad to hear it.'

On the morning of our wedding, she went to the jeweller's in South King Street. Do you know South King Street? Where the Gaiety Theatre is. You've been there for a pantomime, I expect.

Yes to me, you look like a pantomime crowd. I wouldn't have thought you'd be Ibsen.

By then, the public had begun to turn, there were pictures in the shop windows all along what was left of Sackville Street, of Pearse, Clarke, MacDonagh. Must have seemed strange to her. All those pictures, as she walked. And the jeweller asked, 'Can I help you, miss?' And she said she was here to buy two wedding rings, she was to be married that evening. The nice old man said to her, 'But miss, why are you crying? I never saw a bride cry on the morning of her wedding.' And she said, 'I am to marry Mr Plunkett. In the prison. Tonight. He's to be executed in the morning. Can you help me?'

Then the old man cried, too.

God bless him.

He takes out the fob watch. Looks at it.

One of the soldiers who guarded me, a young Tommy, a Londoner, was a handsome, pouty boy. But kind, do you know. You'll get that with the English. I should think he was only seventeen. Glad to not be in France. 'They'd fackin' do me in over there, sir.' From Stepney, or Hackney. One of those places. Mother was Irish. From Leitrim.

He said to me, 'Mr Plunkett, sir, you're an educated man, sir. Wot's it all abaht then?'

And do you know, I felt his question to be the finest was ever asked.

Wot's is all abaht then?

Many answers. No answer.

The people of now will decide that. Not I. Which was surely always obvious. Even to Pearse. To whom nothing was obvious, but the darkness. He believed in the world we can't see.

You tell me you don't? Then why are you here?

He believed in the theatre.

All of us did.

That's what it was.

A piece of theatre.

And there we were: my Grace, the soldiers, the priest. Bars on the prison chapel windows. The *mise-en-scène*. The performance.

And what I remember now is the candle-light on the ten soldiers' faces. I think there were ten. Not certain. The way the light fell on the epaulettes of their uniforms. Strange to be married in a room full of soldiers, all standing to attention, for all the world like a queer sort of honour-guard, though of course that is not what they were.

I was married in handcuffs.

He falters. Fights back tears.

Everything else, I could tolerate. Even understand. *Predict!* But that detail was cruel. My Grace deserved better. To have ... been permitted ... to touch her face ... a moment ... no more ...

(Roars) SHE DESERVED BETTER; DO YOU HEAR ME, YOU BASTARDS?

They killed me last of four of us that day. You can imagine that, I expect. Hearing the others. Not pleasant.

Mick O'Hanrahan. Ned Daly. Poor young Willie Pearse. Then they came, last, to myself.

In the stonebreaker's yard, Kilmainham Gaol, 4th of May, 1916.

The same day the German airship 'L 7' was destroyed off the Slesvig coast.

It's been written that I wasn't afraid.

I was very afraid.

But there are worse forms of slavery than fear.

I would tell you about some of them.

But my ten minutes are up.

That's how long they gave us.

Ten minutes.

Not much.

I am very happy. I am dying for the glory of God ...

He pulls a blindfold from his pocket and puts it on.

... and the honour of Ireland.

The crack of a volley of rifles. He falls.

SIGNATORIES

BIOGRAPHICAL NOTES ON
THE REVOLUTIONARY FIGURES

Éamonn Ceannt (1881–1916) was born Edward Thomas
Kent in Ballymoe, Co. Galway. Educated first by the De La
Salle Brothers and then by the Christian Brothers at North
Richmond Street, he became a clerk in the city treasurer's
office of Dublin Corporation. In September 1899 he joined
the Gaelic League: he had begun to learn the Irish language
from his father and his dedication to Gaelic culture led him to
become an accomplished uilleann piper. His interests became
progressively more revolutionary, however, and in 1907 he
joined Sinn Féin, urging that Irishmen be trained in the use
of arms. Ceannt had a reputation both as a speaker and writer:
he regularly addressed nationalist organisations on political
and cultural topics, and contributed to a range of nationalist
publications both in Irish and English. He was recruited
to the Irish Republican Brotherhood in 1911 by Seán Mac
Diarmada, who also encouraged him to become a founder
member of the Irish Volunteers in November 1913. After the
Volunteer split, he became a leading figure in the new Irish
Volunteer executive, serving as director of communications and
commandant of the 4th Dublin Battalion. In 1915 he joined
of the IRB Supreme Council and, together with Pearse and
Plunkett, was appointed to the military council that planned
the Easter Rising. His under-strength battalion at the South
Dublin Union was involved in some of the fiercest fighting of
Easter week, but Ceannt was strongly opposed to the surrender.
Condemned to death, he was executed on 8 May 1916.

Thomas Clarke (1858–1916) was born on the Isle of Wight but educated at St Patrick's National School, Dungannon and later became involved in the Irish Republican Brotherhood in the town. Sought by the police after his involvement in a riot, Clarke emigrated to New York in August 1880. There he joined Clan na Gael and in March 1883 went on a bombing mission to England, resulting in his arrest and sentencing to penal servitude for life. His prison experience – recounted in *Irish Freedom* (1912) and *Glimpses of an Irish Felon's Prison Life* (1922) – was an especially harsh one and deepened his nationalist resolve. He was released in 1898, after the Amnesty Association took on his case. Clarke found it difficult to obtain work in Ireland so he returned to America where he was employed as a metalworker and as a clerk for Clan na Gael. He married his wife Kathleen – whom he had first met in Limerick – in New York on 16 July 1901.

Anxious to resume activism in Ireland, Clarke returned there in November 1907 and was co-opted on to the supreme council of the Irish Republican Brotherhood. Like Seán Mac Diarmada, he was single-minded in his commitment to revolutionary action and believed all other causes should be subordinated to it. He joined both the Gaelic League and Sinn Féin with the aim of influencing their leadership and, though he supported trade unionism, he was critical of the Irish labour movement's dependence on English unions. Clarke planned many of the details of the Dublin Rising and was regarded by Dublin Castle as the brains behind republican revolutionary activity in Ireland. Secrecy was his chief priority and he hid his intentions from almost all his IRB colleagues. The importance of his role was recognised by the other leaders, who insisted that he be first to sign the Proclamation of the Republic. Clarke served in the General Post Office during Easter week and, although he held no official position or military rank, he presided at military council meetings and played a major part in directing operations. Court-martialled in Richmond Barracks, Clarke made no attempt to defend himself and was sentenced to death. He was executed on 3 May 1916.

James Connolly (1868–1916) was born in Edinburgh of Irish parents who lived among the immigrant community there. He was educated at a Catholic primary school and held a variety of jobs before spending seven years in the British Army, which included a posting to Ireland. After his marriage to Lillie Reynolds, a domestic servant whom he met in Dublin, Connolly returned to Scotland, where he became involved in the labour movement. His friendship with John Leslie and James Keir Hardie deepened his political interests, and their influence can be traced in his writing from this period. Struggling to find work, Connolly accepted a job in Dublin as organiser for the Dublin Socialist Club, and he and his family moved there in 1896. Though the labour movement in Ireland was in its infancy, Connolly became convinced that the best chance for class equality there lay in independence from

Britain. His involvement in the setting up of the Irish Socialist Republican Party and a weekly journal, the *Workers' Republic*, reflects this thinking.

The family's personal circumstances remained precarious however, and Connolly sought to supplement his income by undertaking speaking engagements in England and Scotland. After a successful lecture tour in America in 1902, Connolly returned to work there for the next seven years. Throughout this time he remained committed to the promotion of socialism in Ireland, however, and in January 1908 he established a radical journal, *The Harp*, as the organ of the Irish Socialist Federation, transferring its production to Dublin the following year. In 1911 Connolly became Ulster organiser for the Irish Transport and General Workers' Union. The Dublin Lockout of 1913 was a turning point – Connolly was summoned to Dublin to assist James Larkin, and when the strike failed and Larkin left for America, Connolly took over as acting general secretary of the ITGWU. The outbreak of war and the collapse of international socialism led Connolly to adopt an emphatically nationalist position: espousing a stance of 'war against war' he believed that freedom was a necessary precursor to socialism. His Citizen Army of some two hundred members joined forces with the Volunteers, and Connolly fought with Pearse in the General Post Office. Badly injured, he was executed seated, on 12 May 1916.

———————————

Seán Mac Diarmada (1883–1916) was born in Corranmore, Co. Leitrim. He became involved first in the Ancient Order of Hibernians but was soon converted to militant republicanism. He joined the Irish Republican Brotherhood in 1906 and became organiser of the Dungannon Clubs – which promoted republicanism in Ulster – and later of the Sinn Féin League. Appointed the national organiser for the IRB in 1908, he adopted a policy of infiltrating national cultural organisations. He himself was active in Dublin in the Gaelic League, the Gaelic Athletic Association and the Celtic Literary Society. In autumn 1911 Mac Diarmada contracted poliomyelitis and was left with a permanent limp. He continued his activism however, travelling to the USA as IRB delegate to the Clan na Gael convention in Atlantic City in October 1912.

Elected secretary of the IRB Supreme Council in 1913, Mac Diarmada was instrumental in the decision to stage an armed insurrection during the First World War. Together with Clarke, he conspired to restrict planning for the Rising to a trusted group, a decision facilitated by the Volunteer split. Elected to the Irish Volunteers' general council and, in 1915, to the central executive, Mac Diarmada persuaded James Connolly to join him on the secret military council. In the last critical months before the Rising, it was Mac Diarmada's capacity for covert activity and his network of associates that facilitated planning. Throughout Easter week he remained, in civilian clothes, with the headquarter's garrison in the GPO, functioning as adjutant to Connolly and coordinating the operation of a field hospital in the building. He and Connolly would be the last two of the rebellion leaders to be executed by firing squad in the yard of Kilmainham Gaol on 12 May 1916.

Thomas MacDonagh (1878–1916) was born in Co. Tipperary, the son of two national school teachers, neither of whom was political in outlook. On completing his schooling at Rockwell College, MacDonagh intended joining the Catholic priesthood, but experienced a crisis of faith and chose instead a career as a teacher and writer. Until this point he had shown little interest in cultural nationalism but while he was a master at St Kieran's College, Kilkenny between 1901–3, he joined the Gaelic League and became deeply involved in its activities. He published two volumes of poetry during this period – *Through the Ivory Gate* (1902) and *April and May* (1903) – and these chart his development both spiritually and politically. Though he became disillusioned by the language movement, in 1908 he moved to Dublin to teach language and literature at St Enda's College, which had recently been established by Padraig Pearse. MacDonagh became increasingly involved in literary and theatrical circles in Dublin and formed a close friendship with Joseph Mary Plunkett.

MacDonagh read English, French and Irish at UCD, graduating with a BA in 1910 and for the next two years combined writing and postgraduate research with part-time teaching at St Enda's. He was awarded a First Class Honours

MA by UCD in October 1911 and appointed as an assistant lecturer there. He was co-founder and associate editor of the *Irish Review*, where his second play, 'Metempsychosis', appeared. *Lyrical Poems*, published in 1913, gathered work from MacDonagh's first three books and added new material, including some translations from the Irish. During this time he became committed to physical force nationalism, joining the Irish Volunteers shortly after their formation and supporting their recruitment efforts by speaking around the country and writing articles for the *Irish Review*. Though he was sworn in to the Irish Republican Brotherhood he was not involved in the planning of the Easter Rising until shortly before the events took place. On Easter Monday, MacDonagh commanded a force of a hundred and fifty Volunteers occupying Jacob's Biscuit Factory, which was held until the surrender. He was executed on 3 May 1916.

Elizabeth O'Farrell (1884–1957) was born in Dublin, the youngest of two daughters of Christopher Farrell, a dock labourer, and his wife Margaret, a housekeeper. She was educated by the Sisters of Mercy and afterwards became a midwife, working at Holles Street Hospital in Dublin. While at school, O'Farrell formed a lifelong friendship with Julia (Sheila) Grenan. Both young women shared strong nationalist beliefs: they joined the Gaelic League, the Irish Women's Franchise League and the Irish Women Workers' Union. In 1906 they became members of

Inghinidhe na hÉireann and later Cumann na mBan. They were trained in the use of firearms by Constance Markievicz.

On Easter Sunday 1916 the two women were assigned to the Irish Citizen Army, and O'Farrell was entrusted to deliver despatches to units in the west of Ireland. On returning to Dublin, she served in the GPO as a nurse and a courier. After James Connolly was badly injured on 27 April, she and Grenan volunteered to care for him. Together with Connolly's secretary, Winifred Carney, they would be the last women to leave the GPO. Following their retreat with the garrison to Moore Street, O'Farrell was chosen by Padraig Pearse to approach the British military to discuss terms for surrender. She traversed a zone of heavy fire and was eventually taken to Brigadier-General William Lowe. Pearse, accompanied by O'Farrell, surrendered to Lowe that afternoon, and she later took the surrender order to Volunteer and Citizen Army units at the Four Courts, the College of Surgeons, Boland's Mill and Jacob's Factory. This not only exposed her to gunfire but to the hostility of revolutionaries who wished to continue fighting and doubted the authenticity of her orders. In spite of assurances from General Lowe that she would be released, O'Farrell was stripped and searched, and imprisoned overnight in Ship Street Barracks. On hearing of this, Lowe had her released immediately and apologised for her treatment. O'Farrell remained active in republican politics until her death in 1957. She is buried in the republican plot in Glasnevin Cemetery.

Padraig Pearse (1879–1916) was born in Dublin, the elder son of James Pearse, a stone carver, originally from London. He was educated by the Christian Brothers and, at the age of twenty, joined the Gaelic League. He went on to study Irish, English and French at UCD, while also taking law courses; he was called to the Bar in 1901. Pearse was ambitious and hardworking, and his early writings reveal his idealistic commitment to Irish language and culture. In 1903 he became editor of the Gaelic League's weekly newspaper, *An Claidheamh Soluis* and, in this role, was an active moderniser of the language. European influences can be traced in his educational philosophy: Belgian models of bilingual education were a foundation for St Enda's, a progressive secondary school that Pearse established in 1908.

It was not until 1913, when the attainment of Home Rule began to seem unlikely, that Pearse became interested in the possibility of rebellion and signalled this commitment in his writings, praising the spiritual virtue of bloodshed. He joined the Irish Republican Brotherhood in December of that year. Britain's declaration of war on Germany offered increased opportunity for rebellion and, after the Volunteer split, Pearse remained with the minority who opposed John Redmond's call for Irishmen to join the British army. By December of 1914, Pearse had become director of military organisation for the Irish Volunteers and was soon a pivotal member of the Irish Republican Brotherhood's military committee. An armed insurrection was planned for Easter Sunday, 23 April

1916 but when the *Aud* – a ship carrying 20,000 rifles from
Germany – was captured on Good Friday, Eoin MacNeill,
Chief of Staff of the Irish Volunteers, issued a countermanding
order in the *Sunday Independent*. Pearse and other key figures
were determined to proceed with the Rising, however, and
the following day a reduced force was mobilised, seizing the
General Post Office on Sackville Street as their headquarters.
Though Thomas Clarke was the senior figure among the rebel
leaders, Pearse was named president of the new Republic and
it was he who read the Proclamation outside the GPO. After
six days of fighting, Pearse surrendered on 29 April, in order to
prevent further loss of life. He was sentenced to death on 2 May
and executed at 3.30 the following morning.

Joseph Mary Plunkett (1887–1916) was born into a wealthy
and prominent Irish family – his forebears included the
martyred bishop Oliver Plunkett and Sir Horace Plunkett, an
important figure in the Irish co-operative movement. Reared
largely in Dublin, Plunkett suffered from tuberculosis, and
serious respiratory infections disrupted his education. He
attended a school in Paris before entering Belvedere College in
Dublin, and spent a formative two years studying philosophy at
Stonyhurst College in Lancashire. His friendship with Thomas
MacDonagh dates from 1910, when Plunkett sought a tutor
to help him prepare for the NUI matriculation examination.
MacDonagh also encouraged his interest in poetry, which led

to the publication, in 1911, of Plunkett's volume *The Circle and the Sword*. Plunkett travelled with his mother in Italy and Malta that winter and, later the same year, spent time in Algiers where he studied Arabic language and literature. On his return, he helped to establish the *Irish Review* and later used the journal to promote the ethos of the Irish Volunteers, which he had joined at its foundation. In 1914 Plunkett collaborated again with MacDonagh and Edward Martyn in managing the newly launched Irish Theatre.

In the wake of Redmond's Woodenbridge speech, Plunkett attended a meeting called by Thomas Clarke and Seán Mac Diarmada at which a decision was made to stage an armed uprising during the course of the war. As director of military operations of the Irish Republican Brotherhood, Plunkett travelled covertly to Berlin in spring 2015, joining Roger Casement in seeking German support for a Volunteer Rising in Ireland. Larkfield, an extensive property purchased by Plunkett's mother in Kimmage, outside Dublin, was a base for the Volunteers during this period. In April 1916 Plunkett underwent surgery on the tubercular glands in his neck but attended to military council business while convalescing. In spite of his frailty, he served in the General Post Office during the Rising. After his court martial he was granted permission to marry his fiancée, Grace Gifford, in the chapel at Kilmainham Gaol. Plunkett was executed on 4 May 1916.

SIGNATORIES

AUTHOR BIOGRAPHIES

Marina Carr's first play, *Low in the Dark*, was staged in 1989, two years after she graduated from UCD with a BA in English and Philosophy. Five years later *The Mai* brought her critical acclaim, winning Best New Play at the Dublin Theatre Festival. Other plays include *Portia Coughlan* (1996), *By the Bog of Cats* (1998), *Ariel* (2002), *Marble* (2009) and *16 Possible Glimpses* (2011). She has been awarded the *Irish Times* Playwright Award and a Laurence Olivier Award for Best New Play. A member of Aosdána, Carr has been Writer-in-Residence at Trinity College Dublin and at Princeton University. She was Heimbold Professor of Irish Studies at Villanova University, and is currently the first John McGahern Joint Writer-in-Residence in St Patrick's College, Drumcondra and Dublin City University. She received an honorary doctorate from UCD in 2011.

Emma Donoghue is an award-winning novelist, playwright and screenwriter. She graduated from UCD with a BA in 1990 and has a PhD from the University of Cambridge. She received an honorary doctorate from UCD in 2011. She is renowned as a writer of historical fiction – *Slammerkin* was a finalist for the *Irish Times* Irish Fiction Prize in 2001 and *The Sealed Letter* (2008) was joint winner of the Lambda Literary Award for Lesbian Fiction. She has also written plays for radio and for the stage, most recently *The Talk of the Town* – about the writer Maeve Brennan – which premiered at the 2012 Dublin Theatre Festival. Her 2010 novel *Room* was an international bestseller and the winner of numerous awards, including the Commonwealth Prize and the W. H. Smith Paperback of the Year Award. It was the basis of the 2015 film directed by Lenny Abrahamson, which received four Oscar nominations including one for Donoghue herself in the Best Adapted Screenplay category.

Rachel Fehily was born in Dublin and is a graduate of Trinity College Dublin and King's Inns. She received her MA in Drama and Performance Studies from UCD in 2014. She has practised as a barrister and mediator, representing victims of sexual abuse and litigants in medical negligence, defamation, family law and commercial cases. She has contributed articles to the *Irish Times*, the *Sunday Business Post* and *Image* magazine. She recently researched, produced and directed the film *The Descendants: Memory, Representation, Legacy* with the Bar Council of Ireland as part of the Four Courts' 1916 commemorations.

Hugo Hamilton is best known for his memoir *The Speckled People* which recounts his childhood growing up in Dublin with an Irish-speaking father and a German mother. It was adapted for the stage by the author and premiered at the Gate Theatre for the Dublin Theatre Festival in 2012. A second play, *The Mariner*, was staged at the Gate Theatre in 2014. He has written eight novels: the most recent of these, *Every Single Minute* (2014), is a fiction based on a journey to

Berlin that the author made with fellow Irish writer, Nuala
O'Faolain. Hamilton is a member of Aosdána and has been
awarded the Bundesverdienstkreuz by the German state for his
contribution to literature and understanding between Germany
and Ireland.

Thomas Kilroy is a writer, director and academic. Born in
Callan, Co. Kilkenny in 1934, he first graduated from UCD
with a BA in 1956, receiving a HDipEd there in 1957 and
an MA in 1959. Between 1965 and 1973 he lectured at UCD
in the Department of English before being appointed to the
Chair of English at NUI Galway in 1978. His plays include *The
Death and Resurrection of Mr Roche* (1968) and *The Secret Fall of
Constance Wilde* (1997), and he has adapted the work of Anton
Chekhov and Luigi Pirandello for the Irish stage. Among his
many awards are the *Guardian* Fiction Prize and the Irish PEN
Award; he was honoured with a special Lifetime Achievement
Award at the ESB/*Irish Times* Theatre Awards in 2004. He is a
member of the Irish Academy of Letters, the Royal Society of
Literature, and Aosdána.

Frank McGuinness graduated from UCD with a BA in 1974
and an MPhil in 1976. He came to critical attention with his
play *The Factory Girls*, staged at the Abbey Theatre in 1982.
Three years later *Observe the Sons of Ulster Marching Towards*

the Somme opened there on the Peacock stage, and went on to win numerous awards, including a *London Evening Standard* Award and the Ewart-Biggs Peace Prize. Later plays include *Carthaginians* (1988), *Someone Who'll Watch Over Me* (1992) and *The Hanging Gardens* (2007). McGuinness has adapted many European classics for the stage, including plays by Henrik Ibsen and Bertolt Brecht; he is also a poet and fiction writer – his first novel *Arimathea* was published in 2013. He has lectured at the University of Ulster and at NUI Maynooth, and is now Professor of Creative Writing at UCD.

Éilís Ní Dhuibhne is a novelist and short story writer in both Irish and English. She graduated from UCD with a BA in 1974 and the same year published her first short story in the 'New Irish Writing' page of the *Irish Press*. She completed an MPhil at UCD in 1976 and a PhD in 1982 and six years later published her first book, *Blood and Water*. She has since written more than twenty books, including novels, short story collections, plays and works for children. These include *The Bray House* (1990), *The Dancers Dancing* (1999) – which was shortlisted for the Orange Prize – *Fox, Swallow, Scarecrow* (2008) and, most recently, *The Shelter of Neighbours* (2012). She has taught creative writing at the Faber Academy, at Trinity College Dublin and at the Irish Writers' Centre. She is currently Writer Fellow at UCD.

Joseph O'Connor is the author of eight novels, including *Cowboys and Indians* (1991), *Redemption Falls* (2007), *Ghost Light* (2010) and *The Thrill of it All* (2014). *Star of the Sea*, published in 2002, has won numerous awards, including an American Library Association Award and the Prix Littéraire Zepter for European Novel of the Year. O'Connor has also published a number of bestselling works of non-fiction, as well as two collections of short stories, *True Believers* (1993) and *Where Have You Been?* (2012). His adaptation of Daphne du Maurier's novel *My Cousin Rachel* was staged at the Gate Theatre in 2012. He graduated from UCD with a BA in 1984 and an MA in 1986, and received an honorary doctorate from there in 2011. He was awarded an Irish PEN Award in 2012 and in 2014 was appointed Frank McCourt Professor of Creative Writing at the University of Limerick.

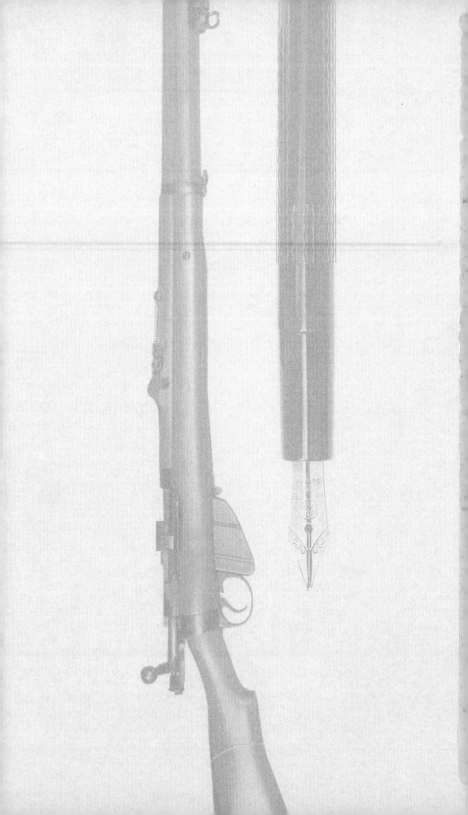

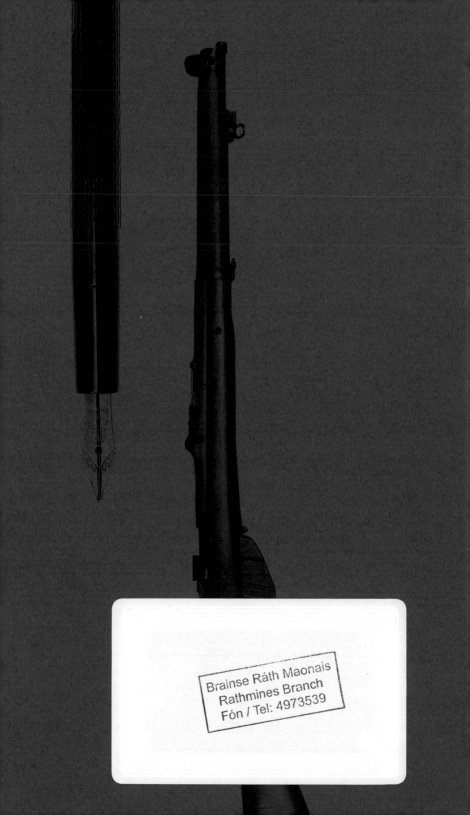